PRAISE FOR DR. JAMES

"James Rouse is one of those very special people who can move us to rise up to our absolute best. In this powerful book, he elegantly offers us a wealth of exceptional ideas that will help anyone live the lives they've always dreamed of living."

~ Robin Sharma, #1 best-selling author of *The Leader Who Had No Title* and *The Monk Who Sold His Ferrari*

"I was so moved by working with Dr. James that together we created a wellness program that has positively impacted thousands of individuals. Dr. James is an amazing presenter—full of easy-to-understand information and strategies, along with lots of joy, humor, and passion. His presentations are enriched by his tremendous knowledge in the fields of nutrition, diet, exercise, and physiology. Furthermore, Dr. James helps people learn how to motivate themselves and use the creative power of their beliefs and intentions. You won't find a more effective or powerful teacher in this field."

~ Dr. Roger W. Teel, senior minister and spiritual director, Mile Hi Church, Lakewood, CO, and author of *This Life Is Joy*

"'Extreme Awesomeness,' is how I define working with Dr. James Rouse! Right from the seven-second hug greeting, to the heart and soul he puts into making his work relevant to the audience. I still remember the loss of a dear one to him a few hours before he had to present to our team in Barcelona. He still came in, gave everything he had to offer. That's a man who truly lives what he preaches. I always remember his words, 'Smile with your eyes.' Are you?"

~ Rishi Khemka, CEO (chief enjoyment officer), MindBox India

Also by James Rouse

Essential Practices
Think, Eat, Move, Thrive
Colorado Fit Kitchen
Not Just for Diabetics
Grow Your Life from Average to Amazing
Are You Willing to Show Up and Live Your Best Life?
Health Solutions for Stress Relief
Health Solutions for Sleep
Health Solutions for Energy
Health Solutions for Weight Loss
Nutrisystem: Nourish

Mind Body Life Mastery
Dr. James Rouse

Be Alive & Well, LLC
First published 2017 by Be Alive & Well, LLC
www.drjamesrouse.com
Copyright © James Rouse 2017

Design: Bruce Pfrommer
Copy Editor: Sonja Sweeney

MIND BODY LIFE MASTERY

DR. JAMES ROUSE

Dedication

To all the ruckus makers, dreamers, nonconformists, delusional optimists, courageous ninjas, warriors of the light, compassion junkies, edge pushers, opulent bubble protectors, art makers, servant leaders, masterpiece producers, and all around kind, loving, and growth-minded Jedis: thank you for choosing to show up and produce your epic motion picture called LIFE!

CONTENTS

INTRODUCTION

Living A Life You Love

You can be successful and happy. Do you believe that? How happy are you right now with your quality of life? Are you tired and stressed out most days, or do you have more than enough energy to do the work you love to do, be present with your loved ones, give to others, and carve out enough time for yourself each and every day?

Imagine your greatest version of success knowing that you have time to care for yourself, be present with family and friends, and give great service to your community. All this is quite possible. How do I know? I am living a life that I love.

I am a husband, father, doctor, international motivational speaker, award-winning author, television personality, and a successful serial entrepreneur. I know firsthand the tough choices high achievers face when prioritizing their time. There have been times in my life when I have been a sleep-deprived, multitasking, over-driven perfectionist. Consequently, I didn't show up as the husband, father, friend, and leader I truly wanted to be. I am not proud of those painful times, but I have grown through the experiences. Now I take care of my mind, body, and spirit first, and have seen a huge leap in energy and productivity.

The Mind Body Life Mastery program will help you do the same. You will become the architect of your great life. You will learn the wonderful secret hidden in plain sight. Making self-care—

including exercise, healthy food choices, and rest—a nonnegotiable part of your daily schedule will allow your productivity to skyrocket and give you more time for the relationships that give your life meaning. Think of life mastery as "productivity plus so much more." Think of it as creating a ruckus.

I am inviting you to become a student of your great life and experiment with this program to find what works for you. Please don't try to set this program up as a massive "to-do list" to check off in a search for perfection. The program is designed to be flexible. It is distilled into powerful, science-based, core body, mind, and spirit practices. The exercise and movement practices are designed for maximum impact with a short time investment. That minimal time investment will give you more energy, help you sleep better, lower your risk for chronic diseases, and put you on the road to a longer and happier life. Perhaps you already eat healthfully and meditate—good for you! This book will combine, sequence, and schedule these practices in a way that works with your physiology and neurochemistry so you can show up focused and full of energy.

Through these mastery practices, you will learn to schedule your workday to get more done while having more than enough time for living a life you love.

These practices have been tested and embraced by my patients, clients, and people just like you. Many of these practices and lifestyle habits are practiced by some of the most happy and successful entrepreneurs (i.e., millionaires and billionaires) on the planet.

I know you will find powerful opportunities to up level your performance and life satisfaction with the ideas in this book. If you are starting out on the road to life mastery, this program will assist you in building true success from the beginning. If you are struggling or have faced setbacks, this book will help you reorient and rebound. If you are currently enjoying great success and happiness in your life, I applaud and celebrate you. The Mind Body Life Mastery program will help reinforce your great habits and intentions and take your life to an even deeper level of meaning and mastery.

Mastery is a dynamic experience of being fully present and proficient with the Now. Now is where you truly connect with your relationships, work, mission, goals, and intentions to create a life you love. Mastery is your commitment to continually growing toward your vision of your best life.

Take a moment to give some thought to these important questions:

- *What does your highest expression of life look like?*
- *What are your biggest challenges?*
- *Are you currently taking care of your body, your mind, and your spirit?*

When you engage in self-care every single day, you expand and prosper so your life reflects what you know you can truly be.

I have used these practices to change my own life. Like many of us, I grew up in a family with dysfunction and addictions. At one time I didn't think I had the grades or ability to go to college. I didn't believe in myself. I learned firsthand the power of passion and purpose to create a life that you love. I went to college and on to graduate school and then medical school. I grew out of my limiting beliefs, and you can too with the life practices in this book.

Using your mind to set goals and have a positive attitude is important, but it leaves out too much. It can be hard to be positive when you are tired and your energy is low. What distinguishes Mind Body Life Mastery from other self-mastery programs? Mind Body Life Mastery is built on what I call the Core Mastery M4 practices: mission, movement, meditation, and meals. As a naturopathic doctor, I love connecting self-mastery to science and cutting-edge research. In this book, I present science-based exercises and techniques that have been tried and tested with thousands of my patients, clients, and those who attend my talks around the world. You'll be studying what I believe are the greatest practices that you can do to show up and express your highest vision every single day.

Here are some rules of the road for our journey together:

Rule One: It's about Continual Practice, Not Perfection

Fortunately, we don't have to be perfect to create a ruckus. We don't become masters of our lives and then we are done. Throughout our lives, we continue to evolve and become more connected to that which is greater than ourselves: our family, our friends, our community, our highest ideals, and our world.

With these practices, I will ask you to commit, roll up your sleeves, and put on your work clothes in the form of an open mind. One day you may be totally focused and inspired. Another day you may not have slept as well as you would have liked; or perhaps you had a rough morning and are not feeling as confident. Here's the thing: Just showing up is the practice. Simply giving yourself permission to show up is what this is really about. Over time, through "on" days and "off," you will find the life you love.

Rule Two: Become a Student of Your Life

Showing up is about being a student of your great life. Study what lights you up, what lifts your energy, and what drains your energy. Being a student of my life has been a game changer for me. Over the last 30 years of studying self-mastery and the lives of true masters, I have created a life that I can honestly say that I love.

I record my Facebook self-mastery videos in my personal retre treehouse high in the Colorado mountains near our home. I call it my "epic living laboratory." I chose the word "laboratory" deliberately. It speaks to the need for openness, experimentation, and being a student of my life to continue to evolve my life.

In order to be a student of your life, don't beat yourself up. Remember rule one: it's not about perfection. You must learn to ignore your inner censor. Take away the power of the inner critic. Remove all negative thoughts from your mind-set as we begin this journey together. Being a student and achieving mastery is all about the practice of showing up each day with an open mind and heart and giving yourself permission to do the things that you are going to learn about in this book.

Give yourself permission to reduce the size of your "but." I like to call it "but reduction," which has nothing to do with your backside and everything to do with what's going on between your ears. When we face any kind of change, we often want to go back to old habits or excuses—something along the lines of, "But I have to work 14 hours a day," "But I don't like to exercise," "But I'm successful because I drive myself hard," or "But I don't have enough time." Sound familiar?

All those "buts" are in your mind. They are based on the version of your history you are telling yourself. It may be something that you learned long ago, such as a false belief that you now mistake for who you are. That belief is not who you are and that's why you are doing this program. We are going to work together to create a life that you absolutely love by overcoming your "buts" and anything else that is not in alignment with the truth of your being. That is what Mind Body Life Mastery is all about: being a disciple of a life that you choose for yourself, unencumbered by the baggage and false beliefs of your past.

Practice discipline. Remember, discipline comes from the word disciple, which simply means being a student of your life. Look at the times when you are most successful; look at the times when you are most happy and fulfilled and when you have the most peace before you go to bed. It's likely that you showed up that day. You chose to be a student of your great life and you gave yourself permission to immerse yourself in the study of what turns you on. You practiced self-discipline.

I invite you to become a ruckus maker. Whether good or bad, moods spread like a contagion from person to person. One person's act of kindness can impact hundreds of people. As you show up as your best self, your optimism, kindness, and compassion will spread further than you could ever imagine. It will not only have a positive impact on your family and friends, it will make a difference to everyone you interact with—from your boss and colleagues to the cashier at the grocery store. Join me in creating a ruckus for good!

OUR JOURNEY AHEAD

The practices you will find in this book are truly transformational when you give yourself permission to be open-minded and open-hearted to the opportunities for growth in your life. You will be slowly introduced to the core Mind Body Life Mastery practices and then return to these practices in each chapter with greater depth as we up the intensity.

Here is the general overview of how I've designed Mind Body Life Mastery:

The book is organized into two parts. Chapters 1 through 5 in part 1 introduce the program. You'll discover the power of being moti-vated by service and how mastering your morning helps you master your life. You'll also say goodbye to exhausting 12-hour days with my time and energy management strategies. You will learn how to eat to fuel success, and I'll show you how to exercise creatively and efficiently. In part 2 , chapters 6 through 9 will show you how apply these core practices to live a phenomenal life. I will provide proven methods for how to get a great night's sleep and explain how to rewrite your genetic script to lower your risk for chronic disease. I provide the not-so-secret "thriveology" sauce to promote longevity as well as life hacks to help you make happiness happen. You will also discover the success practices of happy millionaires and entre-preneurs and create a system that allows you to thrive.

Each chapter includes journal exercises so you can begin thinking and writing down your vision for success, happiness, and how you will integrate this mastery program into your life. Remember that this program is about experimenting with what works for you. Treat yourself to a great journal—one you are inspired to write in and carry with you.

I am on a mission to create a ruckus—everywhere I go. I am a card-carrying ruckus maker and I am inviting you, encouraging you, to become one too. If you're tired of sitting still, playing small, or holding back, it's time to stir things up and create a ruckus. Make some noise. Spread enthusiasm and positivity. Share your gifts and talents with the world. #BetheRuckus.

I am incredibly grateful to be by your side on this journey. We have an opportunity to do something together that is going to transform not just your life, but the lives of those around you.

Qualities of Mind Body Life Mastery

Courage	Creativity
Outrageousness	Taking Action
Optimism	Nonconfronting
Unique	Possibiltarian
Free-Thinking	Inspirational

PART ONE

Mind Body Life Mastery
The Basics

CHAPTER ONE

The Four Foundations of Mastery

Why are you reading this book? Are you not living up to your potential? Is your life not quite where you wish it was at this point?

You may want more energy, more success, more fulfillment, more meaning in your life. As you think about these achievements, ask who else will benefit from you making those changes. Your family members? Your friends? Your coworkers? Strangers? What are the life experiences that would come into alignment with your vision? Playing catch with your children without being out of breath? Having the energy to serve your community? Spending time in nature? Phenomenal work performance? What comes up for you? How you answer this question is where you will become alive and where your motivation becomes sustainable. When you find sustainable motivation, you will be met with wild success in all parts of your life.

In this chapter, you will learn about using motivation, grit, and persistence to create the foundation for your greatest life. How often in your life have you found yourself losing motivation, which has caused you to suffer from not reaching your goals or attaining the life you desire?

You might be thinking, "Hold on, Dr. James. I've been there, done that. I have a mission statement. I've accomplished a lot in my life."

Know that I honor your accomplishments. What I am asking you to do is expand your vision and mission to include the time and energy you will gain from the Mind Body Life Mastery program. When you begin to implement these practices into your life and daily routine, you will no longer have the nagging feeling that you have left some part of your life behind. You won't have to choose between professional success and being a successful, loving human being.

The First Foundation: Your "Big Why"

To find passionate, long-term, sustainable motivation, you need to understand where true motivation comes from. This is the kind of motivation where you don't have to try hard to muster up the energy and the courage to show up as your best self. It's all about identifying your "big why."

The research on motivation is crystal clear when it comes to why you do what you do: when you have a big why, it's much easier to show up every single day to create a life that you truly love.

It comes down to understanding the power of intrinsic motivation, which simply means having a big why. What does that look like in your life? It is understanding that when your "why" is bigger than stroking your ego, you will access the energy, focus, and discipline to make positive changes. That's what intrinsic means. It has nothing to do with how cool we look or how sexy we are or how much money or stuff we have or what other people think about us. It's about how we serve others through our example so they too can have this kind of success and fulfillment. How will being true to your highest calling serve as an example to other people?

When you catch fire, when you are living your life with purpose and passion, it's not just about you. Intrinsic motivation is all about your loved ones and your community. It's about making a difference on the planet. It's about making a ruckus and spreading inspiration, hope, joy, and enthusiasm to others. Because you are intrinsically motivated, you will have epic motivation for the rest of your life.

The flip side is extrinsic motivation. This is all about coming from a place where you are focused on how you look to others. You're driven by money or fame or buying stuff. You end up making your ego the driving force in your life. Studies show that when we're ego driven, we tend to have more anxiety, be more depressed, and lose our mojo because we're coming from the big E: **ego.**

Here's a fact: We are most inspired when we see our life supporting others through our living example. Does that mean you shouldn't want more money, more success, to be more beautiful, or to be more vital? Of course not. Those can be awesome desires; make sure you frame a big why around those wants. Is it just about you? Are you willing to take it to the next level where you say, "If I have all these things, if I am practicing Mind Body Life Mastery, then I can positively impact others." When you can embrace that, you've got your great big why, and you have sustainable motivation.

Journal Exercise: Finding Your Intrinsic Motivation

Visualize what your life looks like when you are intrinsically motivated. Who are the people around you that you most love? What is the impact for them seeing you leading a fulfilling life? Write down your answers in a dedicated Mind Body Life Mastery journal and be specific. Be sure to write down all the things you're looking for when your motivation comes from within. Get a clear picture in your mind. Visualize your responses based on your journaling here and in all the exercises throughout this book. The combination of visualizing and journaling helps crystallize your vision. When you find what it means for you to be intrinsically motivated, you will be truly alive.

Now consider your current day-to-day reality. What motivates you to get through each day? How do those motivators shape your choices every single day? What changes can you make starting right now to move closer to your ideal life?

The Second Foundation: Grit

Sustainable motivation allows you to tap into reservoirs of grit and persistence, which are keys to success.

Have you ever found yourself giving up because, well, it just wasn't "in the cards" for you? Have you ever felt like you weren't measuring up to others, so you decided it would just be easier to play small? Trust me, I can relate. Looking at the academic research on grit relative to success was healing for me. Perhaps you were valedictorian of your class; maybe you had a 4.0 GPA and you aced your classes. If you had great success on that level, wonderful. If you didn't, you're more like me. I struggled with school and dyslexia. Looking at my grades and GPA, you wouldn't know how hard I studied. I had school counselors tell me straight out that I was cut out for vocational training, at best. I allowed that to dictate my performance for the rest of my high school experience. But I refused to give up. I had grit. I had passion and I knew I had a different purpose.

I persisted in not letting self-doubt about academics define me. In fact, I went on to play division I lacrosse in college and received my undergraduate degree in transpersonal psychology with a minor in baroque music. I pursued masters studies in psychology, and I went on to medical school, earning my degree in naturopathic medicine.

This is where grit and the power of persistence comes in. Prestigious institutions such as the University of Pennsylvania and West Point have identified persistence and grit as the foundation of true success. Grit is that tenacity and unwillingness to give up. Whether researchers looked at students or soldiers, the ones who had grit, the ones who had that iron will, were the ones who tended to have the greatest successes. And the good news is that we can actually build grit. Grit is a practice in living. It's a practice of being awake, noticing where you need to do your work, and taking action.

Grit is personal for me in another way. Almost 20 years ago in Colorado, where we make our home, we had a devastating tragedy in our community: the Columbine High School shootings. Like countless others, my wife and I were deeply saddened by this tragedy. And we were motivated to take action. It was a catalyst for us to ask, "What are we going to do?"

I was naïve at that time. I thought I could just make a phone call to the leading television station in Denver and suggest that we put something positive on TV about eating well and talk about self-care to help people cope with this tragedy and help everyone come together as a community around positivity and healing.

So I made that first phone call. Nothing happened. I made the second phone call. Nothing happened. I made dozens of phone calls and nothing happened. No return calls, no interest. I've got to tell you, if I wasn't practicing all of this goodness—eating well, moving and breathing, meditating—I know I would have given up. In fact, when I look at times in my life when I wasn't doing these practices, I did give up. I lost my confidence. I didn't have the self-empowerment from doing those practices day in and day out to help me build my body chemistry for confidence.

Grit is confidence in action. It's about allowing yourself to leverage the confidence that wants to come through you when you support your body chemistry through the Mind Body Life Mastery program.

There are times when all of us have lacked grit in our lives. There are also times when we won't do anything important in our lives unless we exercise our grit. Think about a time in your life when you simply gave up. I have a feeling that if you're reading this book, you have thought, "Gosh, if I could have only stayed with it, what might have happened?" Naturally, I have had the same thoughts. Yet, after 65 phone calls to that TV station, I manifested the glory of grit. That's when they finally said, "Yes, let's talk and give this a try."

We are so grateful that 16 years later, that act of grit grew into the Optimum Wellness program, which now includes TV segments, a magazine, and a website. Our Optimum Wellness program has become the longest-running program of its kind in the history of Tegna Broadcasting, the largest multimedia group in the United States. I give all the credit to grit. That's why I believe it is important for all of us to give ourselves permission to exercise the power of persistence. That power is the result of knowing what our big why looks like and then allowing ourselves to use grit to put our vision into action.

We can actually build grit at the physiological, emotional, and spiritual levels. It comes down to the daily ritual of what I call the Core Mastery M4 practices: mission, movement, meals, and meditation.

Let's look at these core practices and how they will help build grit.

M4 *M4 Practice #1 for Growing Grit: Craft Your Mission*

A personal mission statement provides clarity and gives you a sense of purpose. Have a reason to get up in the morning – a clear goal. A clear mission is a major factor for being happy. Learn something new, stretch your brain, volunteer, serve. Your mission expresses who you are and how you will live. Write down your personal mission statement.

M4 Practice #2 for Growing Grit: Get Moving

M4

Think of it as playing every day. Take a cue from Gabrielle Roth, the spiritual teacher and dancer who introduced the idea and concept of sweating your prayers —this is what it really comes down to. Every day, give yourself permission to move, give yourself permission to exercise. That's a grit builder. As my hero Jack LaLanne, one of the first celebrity exercise advocates, said, "All motion creates positive emotion." High-intensity interval training (HIIT) is particularly effective. To get started, try alternating slow and fast walking. Even just four minutes a day, three days a week of interval training can make positive changes in how you feel. This is one way to build your grit biochemically, neurochemically, and physiologically. Chapter 5 is devoted to incorporating exercise into your epic life. Its efficiency guarantees a minimal time investment relative to the benefits you'll gain.

M4 Practice #3 for Growing Grit: Energize Your Meals

M4

Eating the right foods will provide building blocks to optimize neurotransmitters in the brain, particularly serotonin, which promotes calm; dopamine, which increases focus; and epinephrine, which energizes.

These brain chemicals occur naturally inside of us, and we keep them strong and vital through our food choices. These neurotransmitters help us sustain motivation, focus, and discipline. They are greedy for fuel to work right and they function at their best when there is a steady stream of glucose moving to the brain. Keeping your blood sugar stable helps the brain to keep manufacturing and building these brain chemicals to keep you strong, centered, and motivated. Start with something simple: steel-cut oats with nuts, seeds, and cacao nibs for breakfast are a favorite in our house. Healthy fats like coconut oil, olive oil, and avocados are essential. I give you a list of great foods to include in your Mind Body Life Mastery program in chapter 4. Using food to fuel your best life, all by itself, is a game changer.

M4 Practice #4 for Growing Grit: Center with Your Breath

Do you ever catch yourself either holding your breath or breathing very shallowly? It amazes me what proper breathing and simple breathing practices and meditation can do to change our physiology. Along with diet and exercise, build your grit with mindful breathing, the foundation of many meditation techniques. Conscious, slow breathing is too often a lost art in our fast-paced lives. I believe many things would change for the better if we as a country and a worldwide population would learn how to breathe better. Amen to that. Breathing brings presence. Give yourself permission to center yourself with a breath when your confidence is waning, you're feeling challenged, or your grit is starting to fade. Take a deep breath all the way down into your belly, hold it there for a few seconds, then exhale. This simple practice helps us remember who we are.

Focused breathing can actually take us out of the fight-or-flight response activated by our body's sympathetic nervous system, which induces stress. You help yourself move out of that stress state by activating the calm of the parasympathetic nervous system when you breathe well, when you meditate, when you pray, when you work on being mindful of the present moment. Using the "p" from the term "parasympathetic nervous system" can help you think of the words that begin with "p" that you want to focus on: peace and presence. That's what it is really all about, moving from stress to peace and presence.

Recipe for Grit Building

Begin with your motivation. When you have your intrinsic levers and your big why, you have the physiological components for building grit. Think about how you eat. What foods are going to support your energy and mental clarity? Move each day to build that dopamine to increase focus by sweating your prayers, helping yourself come alive. Consciously breathe throughout the day to maintain your grit and persistence so you can lean into life and create the life that you love. Grit is a game changer when we support it through the M4 practices.

Take a few moments and think about how you're going to begin to incorporate these M4 practices into your life. Stick with some simple choices to get started. Identify your mission, what foods you will eat, what time you will exercise, and how you will remind yourself to breathe using your belly. Write them on a sticky note to put on your computer. Give yourself an opportunity to create bulletproof grit.

The Third Foundation: Building Positive Momentum

I believe that human beings rely on momentum to get them through life. Think about your ideal day and how it begins. Can you think about a time you got off to a bad start, a couple things didn't go right, and that ended up setting the tone for your day? In laying the foundation of Mind Body Life Mastery, it's vital that you understand that how you begin your day is the catalyst for determining how the rest of your day will go. When we establish solid, nonnegotiable habits and rituals right from the beginning, we consciously set ourselves up to "win the day." If this isn't something you already have in place, here's what I suggest:

Start with a "linchpin habit." A linchpin is an essential tool that makes everything around it work. A linchpin habit is something we

25

can put in place every single day so that it becomes nonnegotiable; it becomes a ritual, like brushing your teeth. It can be prayer. It can be breakfast. It can be exercise (my personal favorite). It can be making your bed, five minutes of yoga, or even doing modified squats while you brush your teeth. This absolutely nonnegotiable ritual becomes woven into the fabric of your day. Choose something that you can do every single morning upon waking that gives you a win.

Once you decide to own linchpin habit, take that one positive action around self-care within the first hour after waking up. Doing that one thing moves your day and your life forward because this one action becomes a catalyst for a series of other great actions. With that first win, you will enjoy successive wins throughout your day, and ultimately build momentum for your best life.

 Journal Exercise: Choose Your One Linchpin Habit

Our relationship to mastery is all about momentum. What are a few linchpin habits you could begin tomorrow morning? Write down at least three or four things you know you could do in the first 60 minutes upon waking. Tomorrow morning, when you wake up, give yourself permission to do one of those. Only one. Identify that linchpin habit and crush it. You are creating a ritual around that one habit. Remember, mastery is all about building positive momentum.

MAKING HABITS WORK FOR YOU

Here's something important for you to understand. Somewhere around 95 percent of our behaviors are habits. They are things that we've been doing, maybe for years, simply because we've always done them. When we do things a certain way, the action becomes mindless. We have literally created a groove in our brain. This is known as neuroplasticity, a learned pathway in our brain that becomes like a rut or a groove. If you say, "I've always skipped breakfast," the reality is you have a groove in your brain that says, "You know what? This is how I do things, I can't change." So how do we pull ourselves out of a rut and create new stories and new habits that support mastery?

With Mind Body Life Mastery, you have the opportunity to up your game. You chose one great new linchpin habit to pull you out of that rut and give your brain a brand new groove. Maybe you'll create several new grooves—that's what it truly comes down to. Habits reflect your brain's desire to save oxygen. It's all about efficiency. The good news is that your brain can be rewired. It has the ability to follow directions and adapt to the program that you give it through your thoughts and actions.

Once you lay down a new pathway in your brain, you get the opportunity to identify what you desire. Your brain will start to identify opportunities for greater success, happiness, peace, abundance, whatever those things look like to you. New thoughts are put in motion, which start to feed your brain, and your brain starts to lay down new grooves. You become a transformation agent. You start seeking opportunities to grow.

The homework is quite simple and wonderfully clear: Tomorrow morning, and the rest of your life, you secure a new linchpin habit. You give yourself the opportunity to have this keystone habit that lays a foundation for the rest of your day and helps you transform every part of your life by beginning to do one thing well.

Qualities of a Linchpin Habit

Realistic	Nonnegotiable
Embraces Self-Care	Uplifting
Healthy	Convenient
Action-Oriented	

The Fourth Foundation: A Can-Do Mind-Set

If there's anything that people accuse me of being, whether it's online, on television, or simply being out in the world, it's usually that I'm "too happy."

"What is he so happy about? What is up with this guy?" It's as if my being happy is condescending toward others and we should all find something wrong with happiness. Well, you know what? The more we learn about the relationship between happiness and optimism, the more we can get really inspired by it. Stanford University has done a great deal of research on mental and emotional dispositions in relationship to success and mastery. Optimism is powerful. Simply defined, it is a can-do mind-set.

Optimism is also an open-minded and growth-oriented mind-set. Dr. Carol Dweck, a renowned professor of psychology at Stanford University, has identified characteristics of individuals who have decided to become students of life. They are always ready to learn and don't link their self-esteem to what they know. These are the folks who have the greatest success, the greatest happiness, and they tend to live longer and stronger than those who have a fixed mind-set. A fixed mind-set is really about perfectionism. I like to refer to the fixed-mindset as akin to being "chronically adult." This person doesn't try new things, doesn't believe in growing, doesn't want to be vulnerable because then they could fail or be wrong. Optimism is all about a growth mind-set, and this is where success and happiness happen.

An optimistic mind-set helps fight chronic inflammation in our bodies, which has been linked to many diseases. When we're pessimistic, when we're not carrying a can-do attitude, we tend to create physiological stress on our system and that carries a greater risk for depression and other chronic diseases.

YOUR BEST LIFE PRACTICE

I want to share the "best life practice" that Stanford researchers have been doing with thousands of people. The researchers ask people to write down what their best life looks like in one year, five years, and ten years down the road. I invite you to do this in your journal now.

This can be uncomfortable for many of us. When we give ourselves the opportunity to dream that big and attach our intrinsic motivational levers to it, it brings up a lot of fear. We risk thinking, "Oh my goodness, what if I don't get there? What if I have a limiting belief that won't even allow me to see what my best life would look like?"

When I did this practice the first time picturing my best life, it was kind of lame. It wasn't exciting because I couldn't give myself permission to leverage it to the level I truly wanted. Now my wife and I do this practice every month, and I've got to tell you, over the last two years the visions we have manifested are tremendous.

I can't wait to get up in the morning and read my goals out loud. I can't wait to take the piece of paper, read the goals, and then actually see them in my mind's eye as my life. Know that when you do this practice, it feels good. This vision will become you.

When you engage in this practice first thing in the morning, it will actually help you sleep at night. We fall asleep under the influence of opportunity and optimism. We sleep peacefully because we can't wait to get up the next morning knowing this is the life we're moving toward.

Your frontal cortex, the part of your brain that's basically "in charge," is the big vision holder. Give it a great big vision, and let the motor cortex engage that big vision, take that energy, and find ways to put it to work.

Journal Exercise: What Is Your Best Life?

Take a few minutes right now and write down your big life ideas and vision. Do it for one year, five years, and ten years down the road. Write one or two sentences, chronicling what you see your best life looking like.

Questions to consider: Where do you live? Who are you spending time with? What are you doing all day long? When you go to bed at night, what are you thinking about? Give yourself as much vividness, as much color, as you possibly can.

You may find your censor or inner critic coming up and saying something like, "Hey, loser, you can't do that. Who do you think you are?" If that happens, simply take a breath. Say to yourself, "Oh, how interesting. That's my old self, that's my limited self. That's the part of me that no longer serves me." Quietly dismiss the critic and reengage with this practice.

HOW TO GAIN CONFIDENCE

My wife and I recently moved into a new house that we helped design from scratch. Though it was "finished" nearly three years ago, we're still fine-tuning many things. If you've ever built anything, whether a house, new business, or a new relationship, you understand that the foundation is the key instrument to allow it all to work.

As we look at the practices we've covered so far, reflect on whether or not you have it within you to do the necessary foundational work.

Allow me to remind you of a few things. Sometimes focusing on grit isn't so sexy. Focusing on the idea of your morning ritual, and your linchpin habit, I know that realistically those things can get old. Do you know what I love about the idea of life mastery? We have our whole lives to work on it. It's about the process. Every single day, we have the opportunity to decide to show up and take action. This is where you gain confidence. It's where you gain happiness and optimism. Every respectable study that's ever been done on happiness, meaning, and fulfillment shows that the people who have achieved the kind of life mastery that we're all shooting for have learned the secret, and the secret is showing up day after day. Every day you lay down the foundation and step-by-step build a life that matters.

Review this chapter as often as you need to. Lay the foundation for Mind Body Life Mastery and make it solid. Think about how you can support your grit and anchor your habits. Allow yourself to envision your ideal life. Recognize how showing up and taking action for your self-care creates the optimism for a "can do" life.

CHAPTER TWO

Master Your Morning to Master Your Life

Do you love the morning, like I do, or do you dread the thought of waking before dawn? Make a commitment to move and flow every morning, and you'll ride the rest of the day on the wave of confidence and courage you created.

I am a morning person, almost to a fault. I became an early riser long before I was aware of the compelling science showing that morning people may actually have an advantage over people who sleep in.

You have a head start on morning discipline through developing and practicing your nonnegotiable morning linchpin ritual in chapter 1. In this chapter, you'll discover new strategies to shift your physiology and your mind-set so you can make peace with becoming a morning person.

We evolved to rise with the sun and relax with the sunset. This is the rhythm of the life we are meant to be living. When we align with that rhythm of life, we program ourselves for success, happiness, productivity, life balance, and fulfillment. Think about what your life will look like when you rise and shine every single day ready to express your highest self: world-class living and world-class giving!

Morning mastery is a catalyst for everything that you want more of in your life: energy, success, joy, and focus. Do you think it's any accident that the morning is characterized as the a.m.? As much as

I'd love to impress my high school Latin teacher, I am not talking about ante meridiem, which is Latin for "before midday." For me, a.m. stands for AMazing!

If you aren't a morning person, help is on the way. In this chapter, you'll learn how to shift your mind-set about getting up earlier, and we'll use our M4 practices to help shift your body chemistry to make it easier.

I'm sure you already know that circadian rhythm is your body's 24-hour cycle for sleeping and waking. You may think your biology destined you to be a night owl, but that behavior is more likely due to your mind-set and your previously adopted habits. When the invention of the light bulb extended everyone's day, we not only lost connection with our circadian rhythm, we also lost approximately 30 percent of our sleep time.

Let's consider the hormone cortisol and its relationship to our day. In the right amounts, cortisol carries energy to our muscles. If there is too much cortisol in circulation, it can devastate our emotions, challenge our immune systems, and keep us from being our best. Cortisol works with our circadian rhythms and starts rising about 4:00 a.m. and peaks around 10:00 a.m. to noon, but we lose connection with that when we stay up late or use stimulants to stay awake. When cortisol is managed through morning movement, our minds, bodies, and spiritual well-being benefit. In contrast, if cortisol is depressed or doesn't start to rise in the morning, it makes getting out of bed that much harder. Exercise becomes a game changer here to get healthy hormone levels back on track.

We have an inner pharmacy of hormones, neurochemicals, vitamins, minerals, electrolytes, and more—all ready to build a day filled with focus, courage, motivation, happiness, balance, and peace. We just have to know how to leverage this pharmacy from the moment we wake up in the morning so it can truly go to work for us.

FLOW FROM YOUR MORNING INTO YOUR DAY

When you wake up earlier, you set yourself up to be in a state of flow for the entire day. When you are in the flow state you are in the moment, mindful of what is going on around you, engaged with your tasks, and rocking your productivity. You are loving what you are doing and hours seem like minutes.

Flow doesn't just happen, but you can prime yourself for flow by continuing to deepen the M4 practices. With a few days of these practices under your belt, you will generate momentum that will build for the rest of the day. I call this supercharged state of flow, "flow 2.0."

As we explore this M4 sequence for creating flow 2.0, think about how you can play with these practices. Don't be a chronic adult thinking, "I've got so much going on already. I don't have time!" Believe me, I understand. We've all got a lot of stuff going on. I appreciate that, but this is about carving out 60 minutes in the morning to give yourself the experience of living the life you came here to live. If you don't have 60 minutes, then gift yourself with 20 to 30 minutes or even 10 minutes. With this time investment, you'll discover what it's like to have your physiology, biochemistry, and spirit fully engaged with living.

When you think about your goals and opportunities, consider how embracing morning mastery will help you live an amazing life. Use the journal exercises and practices to break through the mental blocks and habits keeping you from thriving through the mornings. Begin immediately.

M4 PRACTICE #1: Morning Mission

You face a choice when you wake up each morning. You can either say with excitement, "Good morning, God!" or say with dread and angst, "Good God, it's morning!" The mind-set you choose will set the tone for your entire day for good or ill.

Some people like to roll over in denial and hit the snooze alarm. Please don't do that. Studies show that we confuse our neurochemistry when this happens. We are caught in neurological purgatory; we're not in hell and we're not in heaven; we're stuck in mediocrity. To jump start our amazing inner pharmacy, we have to get up and embrace the day.

Once you wake up, ask yourself: "What's my mission for the day?" Be conscious of how you will create your day. Picture your mission in your mind's eye. Reflect on the big why you wrote about in your journal.

 M4 PRACTICE #2: Morning Movement

Many people consider exercise "the dreaded E word," but the truth is that exercise is something that you have to make peace with in order to show up as your best self. If you're not an exerciser, I want to help you to find a way to see movement as a way to be a better human being instead of seeing it as punishment. A short walk is helpful, but if you want to experience flow 2.0, you've got to raise your heart rate. This may be uncomfortable for some, but remember, the awesome results will be worth it! Here's why.
Let's learn more about your inner pharmacy. When you move first thing in the morning, you take cortisol, that pesky chronic stress hormone, and give it a job to do. Rather than marinating

in your cortisol, you're going to put it to work sending energy to your muscles. You are unleashing your health, well-being, and true awesomeness by releasing a biochemical cascade that gives you powerful and inspiring opportunities to light up your life and the lives of everyone you touch. With exercise, you ignite your inner ruckus maker, spreading positive energy all around you. Without exercise, it doesn't happen.

M4 PRACTICE #3: Morning Meditation **M4**

From movement, flow into meditation, prayer, or mindfulness. Whatever you like to call it, it works, trust me. One of the reasons for that is because the stillness of any one of these practices is usually accompanied by deeper breathing. This activates the vagus nerve, which helps balance your nervous system and keeps you calm. It helps maintain your natural circadian rhythms and engages your parasympathetic nervous system, which is where you regain balance, composure, and happiness.

Think of a time when a negative email came into your inbox or someone cut you off in traffic, and two hours later you were still ruminating on it. That's human nature, but it's also physiology. The sympathetic nervous system and cortisol work together to bring us down the rabbit hole where we ruminate and become our less-than-best selves. Meditation strengthens the vagus nerve to keep us in equanimity. Think of equanimity like a homing device to get you back to your highest version of yourself; it helps you get out of that rabbit hole. When we've lost that connection, it's easy to go down the fight-or-flight path of sympathetic dominance. That leads to more cortisol and chronic stress. We end up losing ourselves, our minds, and our goodness.

There is another positive side effect of meditation and deep breathing: it will silence your inner critic. There's a part of your brain called the amygdala, which you can think of as the brain's alarm system. It's been around since the earliest mammals and is constantly scanning for threats. As we've evolved over thousands of years, we have come to a place where sometimes the amygdala overstays its welcome. It keeps us playing small and doesn't allow us to stretch ourselves.

Meditation trains the vagus nerve to bring you back to a tranquil parasympathetic state and calms the amygdala so you become peaceful and balanced. That's your birthright and why meditation is so important. You may be thinking to yourself, "I have no idea even how to do this." Let's look at some simple ways to start.

 Journal Exercise: Your Relationship to the Morning

What is your present relationship with early mornings? What one thing will help you shift to become a morning person? Here are some ideas: disengage from social media after dinner; avoid the evening news; start winding down around 8:30 p.m. by grabbing a book or meditating. All of these things can be effective, so consider how you can achieve morning mastery. You're going to learn to love the morning.

PRACTICE: The Box Breath

Here is a basic practice to get you started. The US Navy SEALs have a practice called the "box breath" to stay calm and focused. Retired SEAL commander Mark Divine, creator of the SEALFIT books and training programs for civilians, says the box breath is an awesome way to regain your composure in the heat of the moment. Best of all, it is simple: Inhale through your nose and into your belly for four seconds. Hold your breath for four seconds. Release your breath for four seconds through your mouth or nose, whichever feels more comfortable. Be quiet for four seconds. Then repeat the cycle. Even if you are brand new to meditation, you can start your practice by simply doing a few box breaths every morning.

MEDITATION IS EXERCISE FOR THE BRAIN

Not convinced yet? In addition to activating the vagus nerve and the parasympathetic calming reflex, once you accomplish about 11 cumulative hours of meditation, you literally grow a bigger brain. Imagine that! You can grow a bigger brain with just 11 hours of time invested. Specifically, you grow your brain's gray matter, which houses your memory and creativity. Meditation also helps the brain's hippocampus, which is all about learning and memory.

You've probably heard that as you age your brain gets smaller. The good news is that's only true if you don't exercise, stop eating well, are under a ton of stress, or are not drinking enough water. If you're not participating in your great big life, your brain will shrink. It needs to be used, it needs to be stretched. Think of meditation as pumping iron for your brain. How cool is that?

Our brains grow when meditation and exercise stimulate the brain-derived neurotrophic factor (BDNF), which is a part of neurogenesis (i.e., building new neurons). Think of the BDNF as Miracle-Gro fertilizer for your brain. When we meditate, we release the BDNF Miracle-Gro and bring our inner genius online. Consider the possibilities for your life when you live it in a more creative and resilient way!

Mindfulness and meditation have also been clinically proven to lower a systemic marker of chronic inflammation in the body known as C-reactive protein. Chronic inflammation is the nemesis of your great life. It makes you age faster and drives diseases such as cancer, Alzheimer's, heart disease, diabetes, and depression. Left unchecked, chronic inflammation will destroy your life, and your last years may be filled with pain and misery. I urge you to get a blood marker test to measure C-reactive protein.

If you want more genius, a bigger brain, inner peace, plus a longer, healthier life, gift yourself with a morning meditation practice. You fight the inflammatory fire when you sit quietly.

 M4 PRACTICE #4: Morning Meals

One of the more common questions I receive from just about every individual or group I work with is, "What should I eat?" I understand there is a lot of confusing and conflicting information out there. All of the other M4 practices can be uplifted by your fuel of choice. For right now I want to give you a preview of coming attractions. The best morning meal combines healthy fats from avocado, coconut oil, olive oil, nuts, and seeds; clean protein from pasture-raised eggs, plant-based proteins, and wild fish; and high-fiber carbohydrates like steel-cut oats, sweet potatoes, and dark-green leafy vegetables.

In chapter 4, you'll learn how to schedule your meals to maintain energy all day, control your blood sugar, reduce junk food cravings, and support your inner pharmacy. And here's some news I think you'll love: the best kind of chocolate eaten at the right time of day will help you positively influence your world!

 Journal Exercise: Implementing Morning Mastery

Begin designing your morning "hour of power": your personal empowerment, morning mastery, and flow time. Schedule your practice like it's the most important meeting of your entire day. An hour is ideal, but if you will devote 10, 20, or 30 minutes to your M4 routine, that's a start and you can build from there.

Jot down what a typical morning looks like. Do you do any of the M4 practices already, or do you hit the snooze button, jump out of bed at the last possible minute, and scarf down a bagel while driving to work? Are you willing to adjust your evening schedule to get to bed earlier? Can you surrender late-night news, television, or Internet so you can be more mindful in the evenings and read, connect with loved ones, and relax? What will you gain if you embrace these practices? Write down some ideas, make a plan, and dedicate yourself to scheduling your new morning hour of power starting tomorrow.

It may seem like a challenge for you to set an earlier alarm. Let your mission serve as your big why to power your mornings.

THE M4 PRACTICES AND YOUR INNER PHARMACY

Let's recap your morning M4 routine. Remember your mission first thing in the morning and visualize moving through your day powered by your big why. Get up and move your body. Stimulate your vagus nerve and grow your brain for creativity through meditation, mindfulness, or prayer. Use your meal to consume the right foods to turn on all those amazing chemicals in your inner pharmacy and create the building blocks for a great day.

The synergistic outcome of the M4 practices creates an internal environment for being a world-class human being. This setting is a combination of the neurochemicals norepinephrine (builds energy, focus, and discipline), serotonin (support system for happiness, calm, contentment, and centeredness), dopamine (provides focus, motivation, courage, and grit), and anandamide (your brain's bliss chemical).

You are literally wired for genius. You are built to be amazing. Flow 2.0 doesn't happen when you are caught up in mediocrity. Don't look back late in life and know that you didn't use your mornings well.

You may have to push yourself to activate the flow 2.0 state through the M4s, but your rewards will be huge! The M4 experience is an invitation to leave mediocrity, complacency, and average behind. Silence that inner critic and ignite your creativity. These practices won't just have you thinking outside of the box; you'll be so creative and forward thinking that you won't even see the box. Grow into your greatest version of yourself. Redefine your life and your way of showing up in the world.

I love the idea of service represented by the bodhisattva in Buddhism. Bodhisattvas could transcend the physical world and stay in the spiritual realms. Instead, they stay in the physical world and become a model for others. Figuratively, they hold the ladder for other people to help them achieve enlightenment. When you engage in this level of self-care, you are almost like a bodhisattva, an enlightened being.

As you incorporate the M4s into your life, you become a living demonstration of the possibility that every human being has to show up as their highest self. You become a catalyst to raise the vibration of the entire world around you when you master your mornings.

CHAPTER THREE

Manage Your Time and Energy to Rock Your Day

Think about your greatest days when your work and relationships are in the flow. Would you agree these experiences are intimately connected to your energy level? Energy is the currency of a great life. You are energetic when you are feeling alive and strong and have a love-light shining through you.

When is your energy low? When does it peak? Is your energy strong and consistent most days? We all have access to our energy centers, and this chapter will show you how to turn on the switch. You'll learn how to schedule your day for maximum productivity while saving time. You'll discover ways that sleep, foods, certain dietary supplements, and all exercise work with your inner pharmacy to give you sustained energy.

GET MORE DONE IN LESS TIME

Let's redefine what it means to ignite sustained creative energy. Creative energy is not about going to work at 8:00 a.m. and blindly plowing ahead for 10 hours. Have you seen people at work masquerading as warriors gutting it out? They take pride in skipping lunch breaks. It seems they don't even go to the bathroom. Wonder how do they do that? Perhaps I am actually describing you!

I've been one of those overly driven people, and I've learned that pace is not sustainable. It may look like those folks (or you) are getting away with being hard-driven and perfectionistic, but they're really not. They're creating inflammation and poor health in their bodies. They aren't, in fact, being very efficient with their time.

Research proves that you can get more high-quality work done in less time by alternating focused productivity with rest. I recommend that for 52 minutes you create a ruckus—you work like a ninja, blasting with lights-on focus—and then you step back, recover, and rejuvenate for 17 minutes.

You may be thinking, "That seems weird. If I take that much time off, will I really get that much work done?"

The answer is, yes you will! Studies show that people who alternate between focused work and downtime get more done than people who gut it out for 8 to 10 hours. Plus, you stay motivated and have sufficient and consistent energy.

Think about this: if you do four 52-minute work blocks between 7:30 a.m. and noon, research shows you will get as much done by lunchtime as you would in 8 to 10 hours of work with no breaks. The key is focused intensity. Without breaks you get tired sooner, and it's harder to maintain motivation and focus.

CREATE A BUBBLE OF TOTAL FOCUS

During those 52-minute blocks you want to create what my good friend Robin Sharma, best-selling author of The Monk Who Sold His Ferrari, calls "a tight bubble of total focus around your most valuable opportunities."

This is not about periodically browsing your email box or social media feeds. To allow this scheduling to work its magic, be with your 52 minutes of creative focus completely and don't allow any interruptions. Turn off your cellphone or put it in another room.

ENJOY 17 MINUTES REJUVENATING

Do no work during your 17 minutes off. Give yourself permission to get away from your desk and disengage. Think of these 17 minutes as your oasis for recovery. Here are some ideas: Go outside for fresh air and sunlight. Snack on seeds and nuts to support dopamine for more focus and energy. Do a yoga pose or some other gentle exercise. Close your eyes and meditate. When you return for that next 52-minute block, you will be on fire with focus and purpose. And your amazing neurochemistry, including dopamine, norepinephrine, and serotonin, are going to help you to create masterful work.

Journal Exercise: Design Your Ideal Day

Think about how you currently design your day. If you don't have a design for your day, consider that you may have a default routine driven by mindless habits. Write about your ideal day and implement it as soon as possible. Consider the optimal energy window between 7:30 a.m. and noon. Draw squares for those four 52-minute blocks of creative work and write in each square what work you will be doing.

Then, equally important, draw your four 17-minute rejuvenation blocks. What do those blocks look like for you? Be creative. Approach a coworker and say, "Let's go outside and walk for 17 minutes." If you work from home, step away from your desk and get outdoors if you can. If you want to mix and match, try a seven-minute walk with seven minutes of meditation and then grab a handful of almonds. Schedule these recovery activities now. As you do this, consider what you are creating in your day. Whatever you do to rejuvenate, it should always be motivated by your big why to keep you energized.

I hope you are inspired to see the possibilities. Program your day to tackle your most meaningful work before noon when you are focused and jamming. Once you've created your master-piece in the morning, in the afternoon you can return emails and perform other to-dos that don't take a ton of creativity. I understand that not all of us work by this type of schedule. Perhaps you are a shift worker or you work late evenings into the early morning. I am talking here about bookmarking peri-ods of time where you can stay focused and avoid easy distrac-tions (like email or Facebook, for example). Carve out your ideal windows to create a productive and perhaps even more important, joyful, day!

If taking multiple breaks brings up feelings of being a slacker, encourage yourself by remembering that research says you will accomplish more and produce higher-quality work. Let your awesome self out to work and play during your day.

SUPERCHARGE YOUR ENERGY ALL DAY LONG

Morning mastery, the M4 practices, and alternating work and rejuvenation will set you up to rock your days in less time. Now you'll learn about the physiological tools to maintain that awesome energy throughout your day.

A lot of folks say, "I could have an extraordinary life if I just had more energy." You absolutely can have sustained energy. If you have a history of low energy, now is your opportunity to let go of limiting ideas about what's possible for you.

There is a biological reason why you were created to have sustained energy. Some 37 trillion cells in your body each have an internal power plant called mitochondria—the body's energy-building factories. Implementing the right daily rituals will make the most of these natural energy generators. Supercharge your energy through the following practices:

1. Early to bed, early to rise. Here is one more reason to turn in at 9:00 p.m.: your adrenal glands help regulate blood sugar and adjust to stress. They help convert the food we eat into energy. They often "burn out" or fatigue because our fast-paced, fast-food, late-night lifestyles do not allow for adrenal recovery. Burned out adrenals lower your energy and increase your feelings of stress. In bed at 9:00 p.m. and up (and out of bed) at 5:00 a.m. aligns with your adrenal recovery window, which supports both your mitochondria and circadian rhythm (discussed in chapter 2). To move closer to shutting down at 9:00 p.m., affirm to yourself, "At 9:00 p.m. I am no longer a human doing, I am turning into a human being."

When I suggest tucking in by 9:00 p.m., I often hear, "You have no idea about my busy life." If that's what you're thinking, I have some great news for you. We are at choice when it comes to how busy we are. We can choose to watch television and surf the net, or we can choose to have energy the following day. We can't have it both ways. Being a night owl doesn't make you a "cool kid," nor does only getting five hours of sleep because that's "all you need." Sorry, I don't buy that and research does not support it either (unless you're one of the 2% of superhumans who make up part of the exception).

2. High-intensity interval training. Mitochondria (the energy-producing cells of the body) thrive on high-intensity interval training (HIIT). Simply changing speeds with whatever exercise you choose will do the job. Interval training will stretch you. You may not love it until you get used to it, but you will love the energy it gives you. I'll add some complexity to the simple interval practice combined with resistance training later in this chapter.

3. More healthy fats and dark-green leafy veggies, less refined sugar. Imagine if each of your trillions of mitochondria had all the necessary building blocks to build energy? You'd be unstoppable! These easy eating adjustments can get you there.

Throughout the day eat omega-3 fatty acids, the healthy fats that are found in wild fish, nuts, seeds, avocado, coconut, and seaweed. Omega-3s are simple to add into your diet and serve as delicious, energetic building blocks. Add dark-green leafy (DGL) vegetables such as kale and spinach whenever you can. If you are a person who loves a morning omelet, load it up with sautéed spinach. In the afternoon, combine a DGL salad with wild salmon, organic chicken, or add nuts and seeds. You can use any type of green leafy vegetable. The more you eat of these foods, the more you are going to have consistent daily energy. You'll also be fighting inflammation thanks to all the B vitamins and antioxidants you're taking in.

Along with bumping up your healthy fats and DGLs, you absolutely must decrease or eliminate refined sugars and refined carbohydrates, which pollute and slow down your mitochondria. I promise, when you make this program a part of your life, you won't even miss them because you will be feeling so awesome and energized.

One of the things my wife and I love to say is that when you are living your greatest life, you are fully immersed in your "epic living laboratory." Laboratories are places of experimentation, not places of perfection. Think about your life like a laboratory where you are experimenting every single moment with what gives you energy and where you are showing up as your highest expression for the greatest good for all whom you love. Truly, your energy level determines if you are a beneficial presence on the planet.

When you have great energy, your epic living laboratory is demonstrating something wonderful.

Journal Exercise: Create Your Epic Living Laboratory

Think about how your daily lifestyle choices relate to when you feel the highest and lowest levels of energy. Respond to the following questions in your journal:

In terms of your lifestyle, what do you do in the morning and afternoon?

What you do before bedtime?

How can you go to bed sooner?

How do you feel when you exercise?

How do you feel when you don't exercise?

When we think about business, we think about "return on investment" or ROI. In terms of food, we can think of ROI as "return on ingestion." What foods do you eat throughout the day? I know when I am not eating my A-game foods, I am not experiencing A-game energy. It's that direct and obvious. I encourage my clients and patients to write down all the food that they consume. Study the relationship of your food input to your energy output. Do you feel inspired, focused, and motivated after you eat a certain kind of food? Do you feel depleted, distracted, and depressed eating another food? Map it out.

You have the lever of change in your hands once you clearly see the connection between your energy and your lifestyle, movement, and food choices.

THE HIGH-FIVE SUPPLEMENTS FOR ENERGY

In the appendix, you'll find detailed explanations for supplements I personally use and recommend to support energy at the cellular level. These suggestions should complement a mostly healthy diet. Talk to your primary care provider before starting any new regimen of supplements, especially if you are taking prescription medicines. My recommended supplements for energy support are acetyl-L-carnitine, alpha-lipoic acid, coenzyme Q10, D-ribose, and magnesium.

I certainly do not suggest relying solely on supplements. Ask yourself if you are getting an energetic return on your food ingestion (ROI). If you aren't, your first course of action is to up level your diet. Then consider if supplements may support you in increasing your energy and showing up in the world as your best self.

AGE-DEFYING EXERCISES FOR ENERGY

Our culture worships youth or, at least, the "appearance" of youth. For me personally, I love "not feeling my age" (whatever that actually means). It is a cultural belief that our physical bodies are in steady decline after age 30 and that aging equates to losing energy. It is true that as we get older our bodies tend to lose lean muscle and we lose vitality and energy. But here is the good news: losing muscle as we age is optional!

Trust me on this. Muscle decreases are mainly due to our behaviors and habits, which are often a result of our misguided mindsets about aging. Some people use age as an excuse not to exercise. Maybe you've even used some yourself, such as, "Why should I punish myself lifting weights or push myself with an exercise program? It won't make any difference at my age."

I am here to tell you that is an incorrect belief; it is not true physiology. People who live long and strong don't buy into myths about aging and exercise. That has been shown in just about every longevity study from universities including Harvard, Johns Hopkins, and Stanford. When we quit living our lives according to popular beliefs about aging, we become outliers, rewriting the rules for aging well. You and I can align with this way of being, yes? We can have lean muscle and energy, God willing, into our eighth, ninth, and tenth decades.

ENERGY PRACTICE: Combining High-Intensity Interval Training with Resistance Training

The practice for having awesome energy as we age is based on a simple equivalence: mitochondria loves muscle and muscle loves mitochondria. This is a beautiful relationship that's important to understand if you want a long life filled with energy and vitality. It takes mitochondria to build lean muscle. HIIT plus resistance training combined takes your energy from average to amazing.

If you're just getting into exercise, consider interval-based walking. Walk as fast as you can for 50 yards, which is about half a football field, or 150 feet, and then slow down for 50 yards. Next do some resistance work such as modified or full push-ups or pull ups. Repeat this sequence three to five times. It's that simple and you will feel the difference in your energy. Alternatively, carve out time for a fitness class and connect with others who are on the path to sustained, awesome energy.

SAVE TIME BY COMBINING PRACTICES

Your interval and resistance training don't have to be done first thing in the morning or at the gym. Remember scheduling your day for 52 minutes of full-on focused work and 17 minutes of rejuvenation?

That 17 minutes is one of your greatest opportunities. During your 52 minutes you are an artist building your masterpiece. Then you have the gift of 17 minutes to build energy and lean muscle by doing high-intensity exercise combined with resistance training. Who are you when you move back into your next 52-minute work block? You are amazing because you charged your brain, body, and physiology. You are rocking your day because you consciously co-created this state of mastery with your body's inner pharmacy.

SELF-CARE PRACTICES BUILD CONFIDENCE AND ENERGY

These mastery practices build on each other and build confidence. How does your confidence feel when you are not living your A game and engaging in the level of self-care you could be? I know that when I'm not doing these practices at the level I could be, my confidence wanes. I become more reactive and not the person I want to be for my wife, my kids, my friends, or Spirit.

We all have off days, but it is a relief to know we don't have to do a hundred things to get back in the game. We can practice a few of the simple things we've looked at in this chapter. Recall the linchpin habit from chapter 1—doing that one thing well can be a catalyst to support you in other things because we are creatures of momentum. First thing in the morning may not be your perfect movement window, but if it does work for you, consider interval walking and resistance training as your daily linchpin habit. This one practice supports your energy and builds your confidence, focus, and motivation.

Journal Exercise: Own Your Power as an Energy Creator

Earlier you explored where your energy rises and where it wanes by mapping out your day and your foods. In your 17-minute rejuvenation blocks, where do you see opportunities to do high-intensity interval training combined with resistance work? Schedule this magical muscle- and energy-building practice in your journal.

You now realize that you are an energy creator and that means you can expand the vision for your life. How amazing is that! Get wonderfully uncomfortable as you visualize who you are and how you're going to show up when you start consciously creating energy. As you visualize your M4 practices, feel the energy and vitality that fill your body. You have the opportunity and the responsibility to cultivate and generate impeccable energy in every moment of your life.

Energy plays a major role in how you are able to engage with the Mind Body Life Mastery program. You are exercising your grit by reading this book and putting it into action in your epic living laboratory.

We have incredible bodies! Our cells are wonderfully forgiving and they want us to be doing the things that nurture them. If you're like me, you'll step back and say, "Wow, what a miracle life is. I can choose to live well." You deserve self-care! It's a huge responsibility to be our highest version of ourselves. More than that, it's a blessing.

CHAPTER FOUR

Eating with Intention to Create
a Life You Love

Eating with intention is a cornerstone of self-care. Most people don't consider eating as more than simple satisfaction and enjoyment. To them it's a task rather than an area of creativity.

We need new ways to think about diets. Diet comes from the Greek word *diaita*, which literally means "way of life," but we've taken that awesome word and limited it to calorie restriction and a list of foods to avoid. In the Mind Body Life Mastery program, we want to reclaim the original Greek meaning of diet as nourishing our best lives.

The Institute of Integrative Nutrition talks about primary versus secondary nutrition. Primary nutrition isn't about carbohydrates, proteins, fats, or sugar. Our primary nutrition is our life purpose and using our gifts and talents in service. Aligning our life with our purpose is the ultimate nourishment.

Secondary nutrition is about proteins, carbohydrates, fats, and everything else. Why do we consider it secondary to life fulfillment? When we approach life with confidence and live with purpose and passion all day long, what we put in our mouths, our secondary nutrition, takes care of itself.

When we're on purpose and living full out at all levels, we will generally crave healthy food when we come home from work, even on super busy days. If we're not living our purpose, we may find ourselves craving sugar and/or salty foods. Junk food is more tempting when our minds are not in a good place and when we have "stinking thinking" going on.

Give yourself permission to embrace true nourishment, a true *diaita*, or way of life. When your life lines up with your primary nutrition—your purpose and service—you can focus on secondary nutrition such as carbohydrates, proteins, and fats in a way that nourishes and sustains you.

We've explored how food impacts our energy level. I presented the idea of ROI— return on ingestion—which is similar to business people focusing on return on investment. In the kitchen or grocery store, with every meal or snack, ask these simple questions: What is my ideal ROI? Do my food choices deliver on the promise to support my passion and give me sustained energy? How do I want to feel after I eat?

Think of your brain and your neurochemistry as the operating system on your hard drive. The software is the choices you make every day. The operating system is dogmatic and produces what you put in. When you put whole food goodness and nourishing secondary nutrition into your operating system, it will fuel your epic life.

Remind yourself of this simple principle: you never eat alone. What you eat is going to circulate your energy and your influence as it spills all over your world, affecting your family, friends, neighbors, acquaintances, and colleagues. Even strangers will be affected by how you use your ROI. That's a powerful idea.

Journal Exercise: How Does Food Align with My Purpose?

Use your journal to consider your ideal ROI and answer the following questions. First, what are you looking for? More energy? More focus? Quality calories that will support your life purpose? Second, how are you doing with your primary nutrition—your big why and way of life? Does food fuel your purpose and passion? Third, you never truly eat alone, so do your food choices also serve family and friends? Your responses to these questions are going to help you set your table for epic living. This is a game-changing opportunity.

LEARNING TO EAT WITH INTENTION

Every time you put food in your mouth, you are curating your biochemistry and neurochemistry. When you eat to support your inner pharmacy, you create focus, motivation, calm, relaxation, and even bliss. Isn't that exciting? Think about the power that you have with your food choices.

I think about this power with unbridled gratitude. When I was growing up, we ate mindlessly for the joy of eating. Joy is never a bad thing, but you know what? In my house, joy came from chips, candy, and junk food. I eventually realized that joy from mindless eating was temporary and did not sustain me.

When we look seriously at our ROI, we can activate our inner pharmacy and boost our five primary neurotransmitters: serotonin, dopamine, acetylcholine, gamma-aminobutyric acid (GABA), and anandamide.

1. Serotonin is the chemical of calm contentment. Think of it as your happiness hormone. Strong serotonin levels create resilience to rebound from life's inevitable challenges. With serotonin you will be centered and feel happy and light. Serotonin plummets when we skip meals, live on sugar, or when our blood sugar is out of balance. When stress and cortisol rise, serotonin falls.

It's simple to build serotonin stores throughout the day. Serotonin is built with whole grains and lean proteins. In the morning, that could come in the form of oatmeal or quinoa. One of my favorite meals is to take a large handful or two of greens (kale, chard, spinach, broccoli) and sauté them in olive oil or coconut oil and enjoy alongside a small serving of clean protein, such as fish, chicken, turkey, grass-fed meat, lentils, tempeh, or nuts/seeds. I find that meal really simple to prepare. When pressed for time, you can combine protein powder (I use Healthy Skoop plant-based protein or organic grass-fed whey protein) with green leafy vegetables in a smoothie. (Information about my company Healthy Skoop can be found in the appendix under "More Supplement Options.")

2. Dopamine levels build focus, motivation, and confidence. Imagine how sustained dopamine would change your day? Usually confidence and motivation wanes around 3:00 p.m.

How do you keep dopamine levels strong throughout the afternoon? Eat foods rich in the amino acid, tyrosine. Choose almonds, avocados, bananas, organic dairy products, grass-fed organic lean meats and poultry, and sesame and pumpkin seeds.

Greek yogurt is a dopamine-inspiring protein powerhouse. Plain, whole-milk Greek yogurt is preferred for lower sugar. If you love sweetness, add cherries or berries, and steer completely clear of highly processed, super-sweet (fruited) yogurts. Researchers at UCLA gave a group of folks a high-quality, high-protein, and probiotic yogurt for four weeks. The control group had yogurt with no probiotics. The group that ate the high-quality yogurt increased their serotonin and dopamine levels. On top of that, they better managed stress and anxiety. The group who consumed the non-probiotic yogurt showed either no change, or an increase in anxiety-like brain activity over time. The researchers found it really came down to the subjects' stores of high-quality probiotics, which increased gut integrity and thus absorption of nutrients.

Exercise also boosts dopamine levels. Try jump-starting your day with a morning walk or workout to stimulate dopamine production, release, and uptake by your brain.

3. Acetylcholine increases focus and concentration. If you are easily distracted or tend to multitask, acetylcholine will help keep you in the eye of the tiger; that is, more focused. Legumes are a great source of acetylcholine. Include a bowl of lentil soup for lunch or consider roasted brussels sprouts with a few pasture-raised, organic eggs over easy. A handful of almonds, pumpkin seeds, macadamia nuts, or walnuts will help support acetylcholine levels.

4. GABA is phenomenal for helping your brain and body relax. This is especially helpful in the evening hours. GABA helps us let go of the intensity of the day. Long-term stress compromises the body's GABA stores. If you don't have enough GABA in your system, your sleep quality may be affected and you may be more prone to anxiety. We require vitamins B6 and B12 to build GABA, and you'll find natural sources of GABA in complex carbohydrates like brown rice, oats, and other whole grains. It is also created through fermentation—look to foods like sauerkraut and kimchi to promote gut health and GABA production.

5. Anandamide is a neurotransmitter known as the body's bliss chemical. The root word, ananda, is Sanskrit for "bliss." The mythologist Joseph Campbell said, "Follow your bliss." Now you can ignite bliss all day and improve your sleep quality by adding anandamide-rich foods to your diet. Wild salmon is a good source, so are avocados. I tend to enjoy at least one avocado every day, sometimes two. Healthy fats help build healthy neurotransmitters. Our brains thrive on healthy fats such as fish, nuts, seeds, olive oil, and avocados. Dark chocolate helps our brains build anandamide. Make sure to eat at least 70 percent dark cocoa content. I love 85 percent cocoa content, but that might be too bitter for you. After lunch, but not much later than 3:00 p.m., is a perfect time to enjoy dark chocolate because it has a little caffeine in it but you don't want it to affect your sleep.

Running also builds anandamide.

 Journal Exercise: What Neurochemicals Do You Want to Increase?

Write down four or five of your daily go-to foods. Do they line up with what you have learned about using food to build these amazing neurochemicals? Choose ways to upgrade each meal and snack to feel energized, positive, and centered.

Be vulnerable and honest in your reflections. Do you feel tired after you eat? Bloated? Do you experience greater anxiety at night? Eat with the end in mind and co-create your desired outcome with your body. You have the daily opportunity to push the button for serotonin, to pull the lever for dopamine, and to say yes to an array of awesome neurochemicals that are going to put a smile on your face and a spring in your step.

Here's how you eat with intention. Before you reach for any food, ask yourself this simple question: What is my ROI? Remember, you are not eating alone. Your food choices impact your home, your work, and your community. You have a pharmacy inside of you. All you have to do is choose foods every day that ignite the experience you are looking for. You have the power to choose happiness, relaxation, and bliss.

When you build your meals and snacks with intention, you absolutely build self-confidence. Start with one meal, or even a healthy snack, and get ready to positively influence your world.

SETTING YOUR TABLE FOR SUCCESS

Eating frequent meals and snacks is a foundational mastery practice. Frequent meals are important for building grit, willpower, and discipline. They keep your blood sugar stable so confidence and willpower flourish. Glucose in the form of blood sugar keeps our brains sharp and focused. When we go too long between meals, glucose levels tend to decrease. So does our confidence and motivation.

FIVE ALIVE IS THE WAY TO THRIVE

"Five alive" means three meals and two snacks a day to keep blood sugar and glucose levels steady. After decades of experimenting with how to eat, I have honestly found this method of meal frequency to provide the energy and metabolic fire that I need to sustain life mastery. It might look something like this:

6:00 a.m.–7:00 a.m.: Breakfast. My go-to muesli (that I've been making and eating for at least the last three years) is a quarter cup of raw, gluten-free oats or quinoa flakes mixed with a few tablespoons of chopped almonds, raw pumpkin seeds, ground flax meal, and raw cacao nibs. I add a tablespoon each of ground chia seeds and hempseed hearts, seasoned with a teaspoon each of cinnamon and turmeric. I usually mix it up with unsweetened almond-coconut milk plus a scoop of Healthy Skoop Breakfast Protein. This kick-butt mixture covers most of our nutrition bases.

9:00 a.m.–10:00 a.m.: Midmorning snack. Something as simple as a handful of walnuts or almonds can give you awesome energy. Enjoy sugar-free Greek yogurt with a few blueberries thrown in to build dopamine and maintain motivation and confidence. It could also be a green smoothie with coconut milk, kale, a half banana, and plant-based protein.

Noon–1:00 p.m.: Lunch helps you build grit for the afternoon. Acetylcholine helps with afternoon focus and concentration. That's not going to happen with highly refined white bread or white pasta for lunch. You know how you feel after those dishes: you are looking at your desk like it could double as a pillow and all you want is a nap! Consider a hearty broth-based soup or salad with lean and clean protein, roasted veggies, and avocado. Maybe a "naked burrito" (brown rice, lean protein, guacamole, pico de gallo, lettuce) minus the cheese is more your style. Mastery means building focus for the afternoon.

3:00 p.m.–4:00 p.m.: Midafternoon snack. Nuts and seeds will serve you well here as they do for your midmorning snack. Check out these benefits: great nutrition, healthy fats, and building dopamine and acetylcholine. All of that and they are so portable. You can have a handful nearly anywhere you find yourself. An apple or celery with some almond butter can also be a good and easy choice. Hummus, carrots, avocado, nuts, seeds—these all are fairly portable and make pretty decent snacks as long as you watch your portions and don't just blindly insert handfuls of nuts into your mouth because they are available.

Consider this scenario. You have a good lunch, but you decide to blast through the next five or six hours without a break, and you skip your midafternoon snack. How do you feel when you get home? You're ravenous. You're moody. You're not the person you want to be. You make a beeline for the kitchen. You're running to the refrigerator. You're grabbing sugar, chips, wine, and you're not even remotely connected to the high-functioning person you want to be. You don't embrace your family because your blood sugar is not in a place that allows you to relate well to others the way you would like to.

Around 6:00 p.m Dinner: When you engage in mindful afternoon snacking mastery, you come home from work more alert, centered, and calm. Instead of grabbing sugary snacks and chips you can make an empowered choice for dinner to help you unwind from your day and relax and genuinely be present with others.

Five alive supports your evening switch from being a human doing to becoming a human being. I'll present more ways to make dinner healthy and relaxing later in this chapter.

GET YOUR FIBER

A high-fiber diet significantly improves blood sugar control and may reduce elevated cholesterol levels. It decreases our risk for certain cancers and helps prevent constipation and hemorrhoids. It is said that 97 percent of Americans don't get enough fiber in their diet. I encourage men to aim for at least 25 grams of fiber daily, and women, aim for at least 30 grams of fiber every day.

How can you get enough fiber to stabilize blood sugar? Look at your meal plate and your snacks. Make sure your plate has what I like to call a "plant slant." Eat small portions of meat and grains and bigger portions of green leafy vegetables. Mix it up with legumes, small amounts of whole grains, abundant (non-starchy) and dark-green leafy vegetables, avocado, figs, prunes, flaxseed, and beans.

Once you have your plant-slant plate in place, add some animal or vegetable protein, but treat it as a side dish rather than a main course. Think of meat as a condiment. If you want some healthy grains such as brown rice or quinoa also treat them as a smaller side dish. I love a big bunch of vegetables on my plate topped with a small side of protein.

Begin using vegetables as your primary source of carbohydrates. When we do this our vitality soars and our blood sugar is sustained. Vegetables have complex carbohydrate fiber and antioxidants that protect our cells and drive our mitochondria to create energy. We can also keep our blood sugar in check with healthy fats. To spark up veggies, sprinkle them with flax meal, drizzle olive oil, or add sliced avocado.

Look at your plate and do a roll call. Ask, "Where are the plants?" If there are lots of veggies as the base of your plate, you're in a good place.

Remember the productivity cycle from chapter 3: 52-minute work blocks followed by 17 minutes of rejuvenation. Those 17-minute breaks are your perfect snacking opportunity. If you can get just seven minutes of walking in, it bumps up your serotonin, and you head happily back to your workstation. Then grab a handful of walnuts, almonds, blueberries, or a stick of string cheese. You'll keep your blood sugar stable and keep those neurotransmitters moving in the right direction.

 Journal Exercise: Schedule Meals and Snacks

Design and schedule plant-slant meals and snacks that will support your blood sugar and brain. Do it now. Writing it down will anchor it in long-term memory. Initially focus on the plant-slant foods you love and that you find easy to prepare. You can be more adventurous in your choices later.

LIVE LONG AND STRONG

People who live the longest and the strongest build each and every meal around plants. That is something that is very easy for us to emulate given the number of pre-packaged salads available and the wide availability of both fresh and frozen dark leafy greens and broccoli. You may be familiar with Dan Buettner's series of books about Blue Zones: places around the world where people live long, extraordinary lives. Blue Zone inhabitants are more prone to live to 100 (and beyond) and have a much lower rate of chronic diseases. Compared to the global average, people in Blue Zones show a low incidence of heart disease and low to no incidence of Alzheimer's disease. They are vital and happy.

What can we learn from people in these Blue Zones?

Their diets are mostly plant based, and only small portions of animal protein are consumed. Plants deliver on one of the greatest scientific promises about healthy, long lives. People who live longer don't eat a ton of superfluous calories, so if you want a long life, don't eat extra calories. The vegetable carbohydrates highlighted in this chapter give the most nutrition for the lowest number of calories.

Nutrient density includes foods that have greater nutritional value for fewer calories. Kale, for example, is a powerful antioxidant and delivers nutrient-dense awesomeness for a small calorie hit.

EAT UNTIL YOU ARE 80 PERCENT FULL

Okinawa boasts some of the longest-living, vital people in the world and the lowest incidence of heart disease. Their meals are guided by a philosophy called *hara hachi bu*, which simply means that they eat until they're 80 percent full. They don't continue to eat until they feel "full" or wait until their bellies are bursting. As population studies show, this way of eating is paying off. You see, it takes a bit of time for our brains to catch up to our bellies, so if we wait until we feel "full" before we stop eating, chances are we will have overeaten and our bellies will feel overly full within about 20 minutes of eating.

Overeating creates inflammation. When we eat with the end in mind, until our hunger is quenched, we can walk away from the table feeling energized. I recognize that here in the United States, too often our lives are rushed and we eat so fast that we don't even register that we're full. Then we're overly full and tired. Presence and mindful eating are the anecdote to that. Eat slowly and lightly for energy and a long life.

EAT LIGHT AND LEAN AT NIGHT

A healthy breakfast sets the tone for the next 12 to 15 hours of your day. Still, I am certain that many of you reading this skip breakfast. And chances are if you are skipping breakfast, you may be making up for it at night with a large dinner. I suggest the opposite approach. At night, we are slowing down and our bodies should be winding down, getting ready for sleep in a few hours. We don't want or need to carry a lot of extra food or calories to bed.

Perhaps you bypass food all day long because you're "too busy." When you get home, your blood sugar is not in a good place; you're ravenous, stressed, and unhappy, and you may eat or snack continuously until it's time to go to bed. What happens next is that you don't feel good. You fall asleep with an overly full belly and your blood sugar out of whack. You don't sleep well.

The solution to the food coma followed by a poor night's sleep is to eat an energizing breakfast and a light and lean dinner to finish the day. Changing this eating pattern will absolutely change everything. Most importantly, it allows rest and mindfulness after dinner to prepare for a great night's sleep. You'll wake up with a healthy hunger and use breakfast as the foundation for your awesome day.

Journal Exercise: What Is Your Relationship With Dinner Time?

Look at the way that you finish your day. Many folks consume their biggest meal at night. How did your family approach dinner when you were growing up? Have you carried that pattern forward? You can create a new habit that will serve your highest good.

LEVERAGE THESE THREE BLUE ZONE PRINCIPLES

I understand that these new eating principles may be a paradigm shift for you. I also know that you can create a new habit that will serve you. The best way to achieve your highest ROI is to start leveraging these three principles: 1) nutrient density, 2) hara hachi bu, and 3) eating light and lean at night. You'll wake up with positive energy in the morning and achieve Mind Body Life Mastery each and every day.

CHAPTER FIVE

Movement for Mastery

Exercise is a powerful catalyst for mastery. I cordially invite you to take your exercise practice to the next level to get maximum benefits with a minimal time investment. You will serve every part of your being: physiological, spiritual, mental, and emotional. When you feel better and have great energy, you are in a position to use life mastery to realize your highest potential in your professional and personal life.

Let's review some benefits of movement.

Boosts lean muscle and human growth hormone (HGH). The number one way to fast-forward the aging process is to lose lean muscle as we age. On average, adults lose between two and three pounds of lean muscle for every decade after age 30. By the time you hit age 50, you could be down anywhere between 15 and 20 pounds of lean muscle. You want to keep your lean muscle—your "vitality tissue"—on your body. HGH is a powerful fuel for building muscle mass and an equally powerful "why" for exercising. A wonderful side effect of HGH: it's great for your brain and skin. It will help you look vital and feel and think younger than your years.

We used to think that declining HGH levels were an inevitable part of aging. Science now shows that HGH responds to our habits and lifestyle. HGH doesn't know how old we are; it only reacts to how we behave. If you behave like a vital, athletic person who manages your life in powerful ways, HGH will continue to work for you as you age. It may be more challenging to get HGH to the level you had when you were 15, but you can grow your body's natural HGH with high-intensity interval training (HIIT) exercise combined with resistance work.

Reduces inflammation. C-reactive protein (CRP) is an indicator of chronic, low-grade inflammation that has a negative impact on our health and vitality. Poor diet, lack of exercise, not sleeping, and generally not managing your life in a proactive way increases inflammation and raises the risk for heart disease, cancer, and other chronic conditions. The HIIT exercise protocol I recommend is one of the best ways to douse the flames of inflammation and lower CRP levels.

Grows your brain. Remember the discussion of brain-derived neurotrophic factor (BDNF), the Miracle-Gro for your brain released by meditation? Now you can add sweating your prayers through HIIT and compound exercise as another way to boost BDNF. BDNF grows new neurons and brings your inner genius online, just as lowering your CRP extends your life. Ignite HIIT and give this wonderful, life-giving protein, BDNF, an opportunity to do its work so you can be more creative.

Optimizes neurotransmitter function to improve your happiness and clarity. You'll be more calm, confident, centered, optimistic, focused, motivated, and courageous.

I'll address the power of sleep in chapter 6. It's an absolute necessity for Mind Body Life Mastery. For now, understand the direct and powerful connection between exercise benefitting your neurotransmitter activity every day and setting the stage for a good night's sleep.

Now let's look at how to get all those benefits and more in an effective and time-saving manner.

FOUR WORKOUT PRINCIPLES TO MAXIMIZE RESULTS IN LESS TIME

1. **High-intensity interval training.** HIIT destroys the myth that you don't have time to exercise. You've had some experience with interval training if you have embraced the movement practices from earlier chapters. Let's look at this practice more deeply.

With HIIT, time invested is almost inconsequential compared to the benefits. Even if you have only 5 minutes, you will reap the rewards to movement including improving insulin sensitivity and decreasing risk for type 2 diabetes.

HIIT is all about shifting speeds. You can implement HIIT with almost any exercise. Walk as fast as you can for 90 seconds and then walk slowly for 30 to 60 seconds. Repeat the cycle for 8 to 10 minutes. How simple is that? Interval work is one of the most powerful ways to help your mind and body achieve physiological, chemical, spiritual, and emotional mastery.

2. **Moving first thing in the morning maximizes your results.** Morning movement sets the tone for a great day. This is a linchpin habit that builds self-efficacy and confidence. A wonderful side effect is that your body will burn more calories for the rest of the day.

I am often asked whether or not you should eat first if you exercise in the morning. You won't need breakfast first if you are exercising for less than an hour and for most people a 30-minute HIIT workout is more than adequate (see my note above where I give you an example of a 10-minute HIIT workout!)—that's one of the great blessings of an interval training program. If you have a giant breakfast, you'll need to wait an hour before you exercise, so a short burst of interval exercise before eating saves time.

3. Compound exercise. This simply means mix it up. Think of the old-school approach to exercise akin to doing a run and then doing something like push-ups at a different time. With compound exercise, you use both of those exercises in concert with each other. Let's use interval walking, or interval wind sprints, as an example. After you complete your fast version and before you start your slow version, do some weight-resistant training. This can be as simple as push-ups or using dumbbells for presses or curls.

Doing two exercises in concert with each other maximizes your body's metabolic support system, helps insulin growth factors, and builds your energy along with other positive physiological shifts. This is taking the idea of HIIT to the next level. You don't have to do 25 push-ups in between interval walking or wind sprints. This practice can be as simple as doing two push-ups between your interval paces to maximize the way your body benefits from exercise.

4. Feed the machine. Old-school thinking said if you want to lose weight, wait as long as you can to eat after you're done exercising, so you don't put any calories back in. That myth has been blown away.

All the benefits I have been writing about are enhanced by eating within about 30 minutes after exercising. Have a small meal, or a protein shake, with a balance of carbohydrate and protein (aim for a 2:1 or 3:1 ratio of carbohydrates to protein and add some healthy fat like a teaspoon of coconut oil). This post-workout refueling strategy helps restore muscle energy stores and helps with recovery and muscle repair. The longer we wait to refuel, the ability of our muscles to fully recover and repair diminishes.

Interval and compound exercises deplete glycogen (stored energy), leaving us tired and sore the next day and lacking the energy for a new workout. When you restore glycogen as soon as possible after your workout with fuel, you are less sore and more ready to push it the next day. Protein helps nutrients move deep into the muscle tissue so cells can repair and muscles can become more powerful.

My favorite foods after working out include unsweetened coconut or almond milk with a scoop of plant-based protein, a handful of kale or spinach, and about a half cup of frozen berries or half of a banana all combined into a smoothie. Sometimes I'll even add a teaspoon or two of almond butter or half an avocado for a little extra healthy fat. I'm a fan of "dinner for breakfast," so I've also been known to have some wild salmon with a small sweet potato and some steamed broccoli.

WHY WE SOMETIMES AVOID EXERCISE

Even with all these benefits and the tools to gain those benefits for a relatively small time investment, some people still find it challenging to follow through. My clients and patients usually stumble because they are hanging onto outdated beliefs that exercise should be hard and take a long time to yield results, or they were teased and made fun of in gym class growing up, so exercise carries a negative association.

I understand; however, if you think small, you'll get small results and miss the great possibilities for your life. I want you to discover a sense of joy when it comes to movement and exercise. It is never too late to reinvent your relationship to your body and self-care. This is one of the secrets to becoming a ruckus maker.

HEALING YOUR RELATIONSHIP WITH MOVEMENT

But reduction. Do you remember "but reduction" from chapter 1? It isn't about our backsides, but it is about all the excuses we let get in the way of living our best lives. In the context of exercise, "but reduction" involves changing the negative beliefs about exercise that we have accumulated through the years.

Some people were made fun of in gym class, or exercise was used as punishment. Some people went out for sports and didn't make the team. Maybe you had a physical injury. I acknowledge that these experiences can be very painful and can build a "big but" as a form of self-protection from the hurt. You can, however, reinvent your relationship to movement and exercise and create new memories.

Are you stuck in old thinking when it comes to traditional ways of looking at exercise? Remember the saying, "No pain, no gain"? According to this belief, exercise meant a huge (painful) time investment. That's where your great big "but" gets in the way: "But I don't have the time." Drop that old-school belief and get moving. You'll love the results you get from the HIIT workout and compound exercise in this chapter.

An attitude of gratitude. Gratefulness builds enthusiasm for exercise. Of course we all have days when we may not have the perceived time or energy for a workout and we have to push or "will" ourselves through our routine. Ultimately, our mind-set about exercise needs to be built on the idea of gratitude. It's that simple. When you can say, "I love to exercise, I am excited to move!" before your workouts, then you'll put yourself "in the zone." When gratitude is your calling card, you will no longer look at movement as punishment, as something you should do, but rather something you get to do.

Treat exercise as play time. The more we embrace the idea of seeing exercise as play, the more we get out of our heads. Whether it's dancing, running, skipping, or doing spontaneous jumping jacks, you can embrace exercise in the spirit of play. See movement as the lightness that it truly is. If you have stopped moving because of age, lifestyle or negative past experiences, step back and redefine what movement and exercise can be for you.

See yourself filled with vitality. Approach exercise and movement as play. Picture yourself with the energy, body, and confidence you desire. Let that soak in. Now think about how exercise has been 100 percent proven to deliver these results. Say yes to improved physiology, to changing the game for your genetic expression and shifting your neurochemistry for positivity, resilience, and grit.

Exercise always makes you feel better. Have you ever said to yourself, "I'm really bummed that I worked out today"? Not likely. In fact, I've never heard anyone regret a workout, ever! Exercise almost guarantees greater happiness and success.

When you move your body, you get a little bit of "nature's Ritalin," the drug that can help those with attention deficit disorder focus, and a little bit of "nature's Prozac," which can help those with depression. Cardiovascular exercise and resistance training help activate dopamine and serotonin activity. Movement helps improve attention, focus, mood, and well-being. I know for me this contributes to my big why when it comes to moving my body every single day. It gets me excited about moving and I trust it will do the same for you.

Ask yourself, "Who am I under the influence of daily exercise?" Thoughtfully reflect on your answer because you will absolutely find what a privilege and honor it is to live the life that you came here to live. Everything that you want more of in your life, that is your big why and that's how exercise can be a joyous part of your daily practice.

Journal Exercise: Your Experience With Movement

Reflect on your lifelong relationship with exercise—the positive and the negative. Do you associate exercise with emotionally or physically painful memories? Have you bought into old-school beliefs about needing lots of time for workouts to get value from exercise? Can you treat exercise as play and bring gratitude and playfulness to your workouts? What are your big whys for exercise?

If you already have a positive mind-set about movement, that's fantastic. If you have some limiting beliefs, reevaluate those beliefs. Don't hang onto a small idea of what exercise can do for you. How can you bring gratitude and playfulness to your workouts? Can you see exercise as an opportunity to have a physiological, spiritual, and emotional outcome that's guaranteed to make you feel and perform better?

Remember the intrinsic levers (inner motivation) versus the extrinsic levers (outer motivation) I've presented. We often begin an exercise program because of the way we want to look physically. That will only carry us so far. We will not have sustained motivation when movement is about how nice our yoga butt or six-pack abs are going to look. As Joseph Campbell loved to say, the hero's journey is about embracing a big why that serves the greater good. What is your big why for exercise?

Reduce the size of your big but by attaching it to your big why. If you think you've got to exercise for a long time to get any benefit or have a painful part of your life history holding you back, then gift yourself by changing your perspective.

Look at how you organize your day. You can invigorate your entire schedule by beginning the day with movement. Set some goals to take your exercise routine to the next level: 5K, 10K, triathlon, marathon, Spartan Race, etc.

TIME TO PLAY

All motion creates positive emotion. Put down your book, take a couple of deep breaths, stand up, and let yourself go for a few minutes. Shake things out. It's time for recess. It's time to set the stage for maximum productivity.

Do a few jumping jacks and follow it up with some shadowboxing. If you're chronically adult, this is going to feel awkward. If you do feel awkward, remember that to be exceptional you have to be uncomfortable. To be amazing you have to lean into the edge of what you think is reasonable.

Allow movement to naturally flow into your day and your life. You are not limited to just doing your morning workout. You have opportunities to move all day. Remember we talked about the energy and productivity cycle: 52 minutes on, 17 minutes off. That 17 minutes off is a really good opportunity for you to move, stretch, walk, or take an interval walk. The ground rule for your workouts is *every single time you choose to move, maximize your results.*

SWEATING YOUR PRAYERS TO SERVE THE WORLD

Exercise is for enlightened living; it's not ego-centered. It is all about how you show up for your life story. This is the story that you want to be living and telling the world. You become wildly awake and alive through your self-care, your self-love, and your willingness to do the great work of moving your body and sweating your prayers.

Journal Exercise: How You Serve When You Dedicate Yourself To Movement

Take the next 10 to 15 minutes to write a full page about what exercise will do for your service to the world if you make it a nonnegotiable part of your day.

How will it affect your confidence and energy as you make your mark on the world? Think about what it means to love and care for yourself so much that you are willing to sweat, push the edges with compound workouts, and then feed the machine with nourishing foods when you are done. When you are willing to be that exceptional day after day, you will gain so much and the people around you will gain too.

I am reminded of the Zen proverb:

Before enlightenment, chop wood, carry water.

After enlightenment, chop wood, carry water.

What does it mean? It means do the work and continue doing the work until the day you die. Exercise is part of the work. Every single day you chop wood and carry water. It will never fail you. Movement will always deliver results if you decide to show up with that level of dedication.

I hope you are as excited about this as I am. You may wish you had learned about this a long time ago. You know what? The timing is perfect for you right now. Look at exercise with a brand new set of eyes and be fully inspired.

EXERCISE AND THE HERO'S JOURNEY

Every morning wake up and ask yourself, "What do I want to stand for today? What does my hero's journey look like?"

Reread your journal where you wrote about what your life looks with the benefits of morning movement. Stand up when you do this. Read it out loud with conviction and great compassion for yourself and great excitement for what's coming as you transform your life.

When you are finished reading, say out loud, "I am grateful for the ability to move. I admire my courage. I admire the way that I'm choosing to expand the ways that I show up in my life." Say it with such conviction that you absolutely know that you are cementing this passion into your brain and creating a new neural pathway to see movement and its impact on your life positively.

Tomorrow morning, when you get up and your life mastery work-out practice unfolds, you will be engaged at the highest level of your emotional, physical, and spiritual being. I can't even express how proud of you I am as I write this. I am moved to know this is the kind of work we're doing together.

Side note: I am well aware that there are many individuals who are physically unable to move. If this is the case for you, I absolutely do not want to come off as offensive or arrogant. I realize there are always exceptions, and I understand that movement impairment can be devastating. Mind-set, physical therapy, and managing stress are key to rehabilitation and life mastery.

PART TWO

Mastering Your
Phenomenal Life

CHAPTER SIX

Sleep for Success

There is a strong correlation between success and a great night's sleep. You may know that sleep can be elusive for high achievers who want to make every minute of every day count. I used to work overnight in television and would be up two and three nights in a row without getting a good night's rest. It wasn't good for my health or peace of mind on any level. Moreover, it was difficult for me to change to a normal sleep pattern when I wasn't doing overnight television. I suffered and so did those around me. I wasn't the husband, the father, or the friend I wanted to be when I wasn't getting enough rest. That is the reason that sleep is near and dear to my heart.

I'm not alone in having a history of difficulty sleeping. The Centers for Disease Control reports that one in three US adults don't get enough sleep.

I've had the honor of being around a lot of people who are highly successful, not just in terms of business, but more importantly, in their family relationships and service to the world. Most of these individuals are phenomenal sleepers.

Your success in business and life starts with a great night's sleep, but getting ready for restorative sleep won't happen by just jumping into bed. You prepare for a great night's sleep by your lifestyle choices throughout the day.

How do you feel after a great night's sleep? You feel great. Maybe you feel amazing or like anything is possible. Under the influence of sound sleep, you become a "possibilitarian," ready to be everything you want to be. You know that no matter what comes your way, you'll be able to handle it. More than that, you will adapt, grow, and create something new out of your challenges because you are well rested.

Sleep helps every part of our being, but as I wrote in an earlier chapter, once the light bulb was invented, we cut ourselves off from the natural circadian rhythms that make up our sleep-wake cycle. We evolved to rise with the sun and relax and sleep after sunset, but now we stay up late into the night. We've literally lost 25 percent to 35 percent of our sleep time. The health consequences of lost sleep are serious.

Heart health can suffer. Absent a good night's sleep, blood pressure tends to rise, which, over time, increases the risk for heart disease and stroke.

Mind and brain are compromised. Without a good night's rest, inflammation increases and drives high levels of the stress hormone cortisol, which negatively affects neurochemistry.

The immune system is weakened. Natural killer cells are the body's primary defense against viruses, bacteria, and cancer. Lack of sleep decreases killer cell activity and depresses the immune system. A good night's rest helps the immune system to be in surveillance mode, looking for offenders that create disease including colds and flu.

Possible shortened life span. There is a direct relationship between a shorter night's sleep or chronic insomnia and lowered life expectancy. Duke University research shows chronic lack of sleep affects our metabolism in a way that can lead to obesity and adult-onset diabetes, which can have a negative impact on heart health.

Sleep mastery is related to heart health, brain/mind health, immune system health, fortitude, and longevity. When you get a great night's rest, you also help your confidence, focus, and motivation. On top of that, a great night's rest makes you more resilient and is also a wonderful buffer against stress.

Journal Exercise: What Is the Quality of Your Sleep

Reflect on your quality of sleep. Do you treat sleep with respect? Do you have rituals to get a great night's sleep, or do you pray for a great night's sleep because you're afraid it will not happen for you? Let's dig in more deeply. Do you sleep more often than not during the night or toss and turn? How many hours do you sleep? Do you wake up at night? Can you fall back asleep if you do? If you don't sleep well, what aspects of your lifestyle might be interfering with a great night's sleep?

FIVE STEPS TO SET THE STAGE FOR SLEEP

The following steps will help you reclaim evening rest to set the foundation for sleep.

1. Digital sunset. When we come home after work, we're often tired, yet still amped up. Television and social media can seem like tempting distractions. These activities medicate us, and it's easy to fall into a trance. Can that be a bad habit?

Studies show that television and social media negatively impact our sleep chemistry. The bright blue light that's coming out of your television, computer screen, tablet, or smartphone tells your pineal gland it's still daylight, so it may not produce adequate melatonin. Melatonin is the chemical that drives a great night's sleep; without it we don't sleep. Even if we manage to fall asleep, we won't sleep well. The more we expose ourselves to electronics in the evening, the more our pineal gland doesn't realize it is nighttime. You can help the pineal gland by darkening your rooms, creating a digital sunset by turning off your screens, dimming the lights, and cultivating the lost art of rest. Try to keep your evening social media surfing to no more than 20 minutes and evening television viewing to an hour or less.

If you are feeling very brave, I invite you to consider a complete media fast. Facebook and mindless television can be incredibly addictive. Studies show that too much television or social media can create depression and anxiety. A media fast may be difficult, but it's a game changer. In lieu of social media or television, read or connect at a meaningful level with a loved one. Spend time journaling or reading an actual book (like this one). Evening rest is the foundation for a great night's sleep and will work synergistically with the practices that follow.

2. Eat a light dinner. To rest in the evening and sleep through the night, follow the Mind Body Life Mastery eating plan in chapter 4, which includes making breakfast your biggest meal of the day and dinner your lightest meal. This will keep your blood sugar balanced and help keep calming serotonin levels strong throughout the day. The strong serotonin levels will then directly influence your melatonin levels at night, setting you up for rest and sleep.

3. A second-wind workout. My good friend and mentor Robin Sharma, author of the best-selling book The Monk Who Sold His Ferrari, advocates a second-wind workout. After dinner go for a slow, short walk, enjoy some light yoga, or do some simple stretching. Whatever positive or negative events happened during your day, learn to shake it off with gentle exercise. This simple practice will help lower your cortisol. It also helps you place a bookend at the end of the day between the part of you that's the productive human doing all day and the connected, loving human being you want to become in the evening.

4. Stick to your bedtime. Sleep is a learned biochemical pattern. For deeply restorative sleep create a habitual bedtime that you stick to seven nights a week. It is critically important to train your brain and body by making this a linchpin habit. Once you've established this habit, your body will realize "9:00 p.m. is the time I go to bed," and it will start to prepare biochemically for sleep.

This is your opportunity to prioritize an optimal bedtime between 9:00 p.m. and 10:00 p.m. Remember the adrenal gland recovery window is between 9:00 p.m. and 5:00 a.m. Be as close to that eight-hour window as you can when picking your bedtime and your wake-up time.

5. The power of gratitude. An attitude of gratitude increases well-being and improves both the duration and quality of sleep. Take a few minutes before you go to bed and write in your journal about five things that you're grateful for that day. It can be simple things like a great connection with a friend at work or that you got out of bed that morning. We too easily take these things for granted, but bringing mindfulness to all the blessings in our life helps us on many levels, including bringing us peace.

Christian D. Larson wrote "The Optimist Creed" in 1912 and its wisdom still endures. To paraphrase one of its points, we want to be so focused on improving ourselves when we show up and serve that we have no time or energy left over at the end of the day to criticize anyone else. That is the essence of gratitude: when you are so gratefully absorbed in creating a ruckus and working on your self mastery, you have no time or energy left to criticize others.

Journal Exercise: Incorporating the Five Steps to Get a Great Sleep

Write down the five steps discussed above. Which steps bring up the most resistance for you?

A digital sunset is as simple as saying, "I am going to give myself this much time for television and digital devices at night and stick to it." Commit to that time limit and put it in your schedule. Can you do a complete media fast even for a day or two? What about a week or two? If you do, you'll watch your sleep dramatically improve.

Do you eat a good breakfast? Do you eat a balanced lunch? Does your midafternoon snack keep your blood sugar stable so you can eat earlier and lighter at night, or are you most hungry at night?

Now think about how you can make some of these steps a reality in your life. Can you incorporate 5 or 10 minutes for a second-wind workout in the early evening to give yourself a rest from the stress and thus bookend your day, moving from a human doing to a human being?

Schedule your nonnegotiable bedtime. When will you get up in the morning? Can you crawl in bed with a great book half an hour before your bedtime to help yourself wind down? Of course you can! It just requires discipline and you are absolutely worth the effort.

Next, write down five things that you're grateful for in your life. Gratitude is a sleep elixir that will help your brain and body and envelop your entire being. Mastery will unfold in you as you rest and restore.

SIMPLE FOOD CHOICES TO PREPARE FOR SLEEP

Good food choices are one tool to create the body chemistry for harmonious sleep. These delicious and commonsense solutions help us avoid the biochemicals and hormones that keep us from sleeping well.

Decrease sugar at night. The more we eat sugar at night, the more we disrupt our sleep chemistry due to the rise and fall of blood sugar. Have you ever crashed on the bed, fallen asleep immediately, and then three hours later you woke up and had trouble going back to sleep? That can be the effect of imbalanced blood sugar. Stop eating dessert after dinner, and if you still crave a little something before bedtime, consider a small bowl of oatmeal with a tablespoon of walnuts and a few dried tart cherries.

A word to the wise: alcohol converts rapidly to sugar and overdoing alcohol at night will get in the way of your sleep chemistry. If you're going to enjoy a glass of wine, have a handful of almonds or walnuts to help keep blood sugar balanced and avoid a huge insulin spike.

Make vitamin B6 part of your evening. B6 is a building block for healthy sleep chemistry. B-complex supplements can sometimes be helpful, but at night B-complex supplements can be overstimulating. Instead, eat food-based B6 sources including wild fish, such as halibut or salmon, and green leafy vegetables for dinner.

Magnesium is a key mineral for sleep. Maintain your magnesium stores throughout the day. Food-based sources include quinoa, brown rice, and oats. In the evening, have a small serving of grains, ideally gluten-free. To get a healthy dose of magnesium from grains, eat whole grains instead of processed or refined grains. If you're a person who doesn't eat grains at all, you can supplement with magnesium at night. I recommend 400 mg (milligrams) to

500 mg per day of magnesium glycinate chelate divided in two doses of 200 mg to 250 mg for morning and night.

Green lettuce. Two things happen when we eat green lettuce: a salad with lettuce before dinner helps us eat fewer calories at night, and green lettuce has a small amount of a natural sedative, lactucarium, which helps promote relaxation.

Natural sources of melatonin. Remember melatonin is released by your pineal gland in combination with darkness and is your primary sleep driver. Dry, unsweetened tart cherries, or unsweetened tart cherry juice, and walnuts provide a bit of natural melatonin. Melatonin supplements may be one route, but if you're interested in using natural foods to support sleep, try six to eight ounces of tart cherry juice in the early evening hours or a handful of dried tart cherries. (To avoid waking up for a bathroom trip, don't drink the cherry juice too close to bedtime.)

Walnuts also contain melatonin and are a wonderful source of healthy fats and fiber. If you want a little sleep snack, try a combination of oatmeal mixed with a small amount of walnuts and dried tart cherries to give you magnesium and the two food-based melatonin sources to support sleep. (This can also help with sugar cravings as mentioned above.)

Understand that from the time you wake up to the time you go to bed, you are either building or sabotaging your sleep chemistry. Sleep chemistry is built all day long through healthy food and lifestyle choices.

Building Blocks for Sleep Mastery:
Morning movement
Balanced blood sugar throughout the day
No caffeine past 3:00 p.m.
Second-wind workout
Digital sunset
Gratitude journaling
Mindfulness meditation

Journal Exercise: Act to Build Confidence for Sleep

What are your current evening go-to foods? If they don't support rest and sleep, plan a food makeover to support a great night's sleep. When you implement these choices into your daily diet plan, you will build confidence and self-efficacy. In addition, pick at least one other practice (meditation, journaling) that you've learned in this chapter and put it into action. Taking action gives you peace of mind, which helps you get a wonderful night's rest.

Dedicating yourself to self-love and self-care for a great night's sleep will help you serve the world at a phenomenal level.

CHAPTER SEVEN

You Are Not Limited by Genetics

We all come into the world with a genetic blueprint. We can choose an unhealthy lifestyle and let our genetic blueprint express as it is, or we can modify that blueprint and thrive with a healthy lifestyle. Epigenetics prove that our mind-sets and environments have a lot to do with how our genes express. Isn't that cool to think about? You have the ability to choose how your genes express themselves.

Genetics is an important topic to me. My own family history includes addiction, heart disease, and depression, which all have genetic components. That history could have set me up for a less-than-healthy experience depending on how my genes expressed themselves.

But my family's genetic history also inspired me to deeply research the emerging science of epigenetics. "Epi" means "above," so we can think of epigenetics as living above our genes. Epigenetics research shows that we can "switch on" health-promoting genes and "switch off" disease-promoting genes. That's good news because many of us have scary conditions in our family histories. Alzheimer's disease, cancer, heart disease, diabetes, depression—whatever your family history may include, you are going to love learning that you are not limited by your genetics or family history.

Life hacks are strategies and techniques that make your life more efficient. In this chapter we'll focus on gene hacks as ways to use simple lifestyle medicine protocols to express something much, much greater for your genes and life.

 Journal Exercise: Your Family History

Consider your family history. Think about your parents and your grandparents and what diseases they had. What do you think you are at risk for? Write it down in your journal. Keep your responses in mind as you read this chapter and learn how to modify disease risks. I realize many of us are not privy to this information. What do you believe your current lifestyle puts you at risk for? What was your environment growing up? How would you rewrite that history if you could?

We all carry a certain genetic blueprint, but whether or not our genes fully express diseases comes down to a lot of things that we can impact through our choices. When our diets, lifestyles, environments, and relationships are aligned with self-care, we can, more often than not, prevent our genes from repeating our inherited history. Remember how we build confidence and optimism? We build it through taking action. This is no different. I am going to examine the habits that will allow you to live above your genetic history and express your best life. Epigenetics hold the key to living your best life.

EPIGENETICALLY AWESOME PRACTICES

There are four practices that can give our genes a new story to tell, and you have already been using three of them in the Mind Body Life Mastery system: exercise, nutrition, and mindfulness. To give our genes all they need to thrive, I will add another key component: assessing our environments and avoiding toxins. These practices will empower you to make lifestyle choices that support your epigenetic expression. This should make you feel liberated. The sky is the limit to how we can help ourselves express all kinds of awesomeness in our lives.

Movement and Your Genes

All movement can be a powerful modifier for your genes. Research suggests that short bursts of exercise, such as the interval training mixed with resistance training I presented in chapter 5, reduce inflammation, which benefits genetic expression. Changing speeds and intensity for shorter time periods tends to be anti-inflammatory, while running for hours and hours tends to increase inflammation in the body. Endurance athletes often do interval training in between long events, which helps build their endurance and overall performance.

I am not suggesting people stop doing marathons or ultramarathons altogether, rather, be mindful of the stress it definitely puts on your body. As far as today's research shows, interval training seems to be the best way to go in terms of helping to modify the inflammatory response and, at the same time, support your highest genetic expression.

Nutrition and Your Genes

The right foods are phenomenal for taking advantage of the findings from epigenetic science. Don't worry, this doesn't mean living on only kale for the rest of your life. Yes, kale might be a staple, but variety and moderation are key, too.

The more plant based our diets are, the more they are rich in supercharged antioxidants including polyphenols and phytochemicals. These plant-based nutrients modify the way our genes express. In general, a plant-based diet gives us a lower calorie hit. Studies show higher calories from steak and ice cream not only increase inflammation and make our genes unhappy, they also increase the likelihood of lifestyle-related diseases.

The Environment and Your Genes

The obvious choices here are to steer clear of pollution, poor-quality drinking water, and pesticide-ridden foods. Keeping away from these toxins has a profoundly positive impact on your genes. What may be less obvious are the people who surround you all day and the quality of those relationships. Toxic relationships can have a powerfully negative effect on your genes.

Media and especially television news has a negative impact on our genes. The more we're told about all the awful things going on in the world, the more we are stressed, fearful, and marinating in the stress hormone cortisol. That is a recipe for increasing inflammation, making our genes unhappy, and accelerating aging.

How do you deal with this? Examine your life and think about the people with whom you feel good when you're around and those who are toxic. Similarly, are your present habits, like watching the news, helpful or damaging to your well-being?

Mindfulness and Your Genes

More than 30 years ago, I knew I wasn't happy. My character and my peace of mind were suffering. I changed my habits. As a young man in my early 20s, I went from heavy partier to spiritual seeker. I gave up the booze and other undesirable substances and began studying transpersonal psychology. I moved into a community of like-minded, health-conscious spiritual seekers, and I began to heal my past.

I know it can be both liberating and sad to do real due diligence, to do our research on our history, and then look forward and ask, "What's the direction I am going based on my current choices and my state of mind?" These are big questions to ask to determine whether your genes will express health or disease. Are your choices really supporting the way that you want to show up every day? How can you find what is and what is not in alignment with your heart and spirit? How can you courageously prune away all that is not aligned with what you want to be standing for?

Positive emotion helps our genes be happy. Daily self-care practices help us feel optimistic and positive and grow our happiness though self-efficacy because they require us to take action. By taking action on what matters, we increase our happiness. Chapter 9 will look at why it's critical to choose happiness and how science and spirituality can contribute to creating more happiness in our lives.

From a spiritual standpoint, one of the greatest ways that we get a chance to affect our genes is through mindfulness. Make a pact with yourself that you're going to be more mindful throughout the day. When you drive to work you may be on "autopilot." Try being more mindful and present during your drive. When you do the dishes after dinner, focus solely on doing the dishes. This may sound silly. It did to me at first because I had subscribed to the school of multitasking. In my head, I was obviously getting more done if I had 22 jobs in a year and could do several things at once. I felt like I was being a productivity superstar, but it was an illusion. When we are mindful, our genes express greater health and vitality and we get more done.

We all have to look at our lives and evaluate how mindful and present we are. Do we give ourselves permission to be right here and now or are we mailing it in? Are we on autopilot? Are we being mindless to avoid feeling overwhelmed?

Even being aware of how you breathe during the day is an awesome practice for letting your genes express at their highest and best. Deep belly breaths help lower inflammation, cortisol, and anxiety. Make checking in with your breathing throughout the day a priority in your epic living laboratory, especially when you find yourself stressed. Does stress bring up shallow breathing? Shallow breathing can negatively impact your genetic expression and fast-forward aging. When you notice shallow breathing, simply take a deep belly breath.

I've focused on the positive side effects of meditation: lower stress hormones and building the strength of your vagus nerve. In addition to these awesome benefits, now you can add meditation's direct, positive effect on your genes. That's a win-win-win!

 Journal Exercise: Make Time for These Four Practices

Set a specific and achievable intention for each of these practices: exercise, nutrition, assessing your environment, and mindfulness.

For each practice write down one thing that you are currently doing that doesn't support your highest good. Then identify one new positive habit in each of these areas. How are you going to make that one shift? We talked about the linchpin habit—giving yourself one goal to meet and building on that momentum. This is an opportunity to build momentum for healthy gene expression.

Here's a simple example: Set a goal to increase your workouts from three times a week to five times a week. Then you can make that success habit truly exceptional by adding an after-work or after-dinner walk. You don't have to work up a sweat after dinner. You'll get lots of benefits from just walking, allowing those stress hormones to dissipate, and creating the space to shift from being a human doing to becoming a human being.

Think about how you can upgrade your environment today. What are you surrounding yourself with? What can you change? For example, cutting television time by half is a phenomenal upgrade. Taking even a week off from all media can be a game changer.

Are you supporting your happiness and activating your vagus nerve with frequent deep, stress-relieving breaths or meditation? Are you in the present or ruminating about the past or worried about the future?

Try this experiment: Tomorrow morning on your commute to work (or taking your child[ren] to school), give yourself permission to just be present. Simply drive or ride public transportation—without multitasking, texting, or talking on the phone. Being present even for five minutes will be a huge shift.

Think about the possibilities and write down the four new things you will do to rise above your genes and create a phenomenal experience for yourself. Think about the impact you're going to have on people you love and even strangers. Be sure not to skip the journal exercises. The level of thought required to write your reflections is critical to your success.

SUPPLEMENTS TO SUPPORT YOUR GENES

In the appendix, you'll find detailed information about my favorite supplements to support your highest genetic expression. These recommended supplements are omega-3 fatty acids, ashwagandha, turmeric, vitamin D3, and Quercetin.

CHAPTER EIGHT

Thrive through the Decades

Living long requires a mastery mind-set for the rest of your life. No matter what your age, this chapter should interest you because it's not only about aging well or living to 100. It's about the quality of the choices you make every single day of your life. Your opportunity to live a long, healthy life depends on your daily habits, rituals, and mind-sets.

Let's consider recent findings about telomeres, which are sequences of DNA at the end of your chromosomes. Telomeres are like shock absorbers for your chromosomes. When they are longer, you get greater shock absorbency and you enable your DNA the opportunity to express more health and vitality as you age. If this bumper is smaller, you have less ability to withstand the stresses and shocks of daily nutritional, emotional, or environmental challenges. Shorter telomeres can mean shorter life expectancy.

If your parents' and grandparents' genetic blueprints and telomeres didn't fare so well, know that you can shift the game for yourself and how you age.

Telomeres are considered an index for the age of your cells. You may be chronologically 25, 45, or 65 years old, but your cells will tell a different story based on the length of your telomeres. Say you are 45 and your telomeres are shorter. Your cells may think they are twice your age, which may impact your performance in work and life in addition to your longevity. You will be less able to absorb the shocks of your current lifestyle. You can also be subject to autoimmune diseases and other immune system challenges.

The good news is there are simple and empowering things you can do every day to help your telomeres and protect your DNA.

 Journal Exercise: Learning from Your Family Tree

Draw a column for your mom and your dad and another for your grandmothers and your grandfathers. How long did they live (or are they still living)? Write down some of their habits. Did(do) they eat lots of sugar? Did (do) they drink alcohol? Did(do) they exercise? Did (do) they have a wide circle of friends? Did (do) they have an abundance or scarcity mind-set? All of these things can affect telomere health. Which habits do you know weren't necessarily the best things for their health? Did you adopt any of their bad habits? What can you do differently?

IMPROVE THE QUALITY OF YOUR LIFE NOW

I've coached people all over the world. Young people often ask me, "Do I really need to be thinking about longevity? That's 30 or 40 years away for me." Telomere health isn't just about how long you're going to live, it's also about how strong you will live now.

Let this message wash over your mind and heart. You have an opportunity to rewrite the script for aging while improving the quality of your life right here and now. And you can do it with simple daily habits and the essentials of thriving—"thriveology"—a system that will serve you for your entire life.

There is too much emphasis on wealth when we think about success in our society. Stuff and money can be wonderful, but only if they are integrated with our physical, emotional, and spiritual health and well-being. We can create an abundance of joy in our lives beyond the material. That's when our telomeres will express health and vitality.

When I was a boy, one of the things that I would live for was to hear my mom or dad say, "We are proud of you." I went to bed feeling peaceful and happy. That parental support may not have been part of your story, but you can do that for yourself now. Think about what you accomplished during the day. What did you stand for? What authenticity and courage did you live from? How did you create a ruckus? You have the opportunity every day to tell yourself, "Great job today, I am proud of you."

WHAT SHORTENS TELOMERES?

1. Not living in alignment with your highest integrity. You have high integrity when your thoughts, actions, and vision are aligned. Being out of alignment creates stress at a cellular level that will fast-forward aging. Look at your life and see what areas are not in integrity. This is about observation, not self-judgment. That's a key distinction. Mindfully observe where you may be stressed from not living your life to fully reflect who you are and what you want to be standing for.

2. Sugar, refined carbohydrates, and junk food. These nutritional "bad boys" damage your telomeres, making you less resilient to stress. Do you medicate stress by reaching for sugar? Are there certain times of the day when stress is more prevalent? How do you deal with those times? A lot of us reach for sugar because when we are stressed, our serotonin levels decrease. When our serotonin levels go down, our happiness decreases, and we look for a quick fix physiologically and emotionally. Sugar is that quick fix but it is not sustainable. Long term, sugar damages the length of your telomeres.

3. Smoking, emotional and environmental stress. Smoking will absolutely age you. It ages your skin and every cell of your being. It also ages your spirit. I apologize if this sounds judgmental. Have you ever noticed when people are sitting or standing outside of their place of work or other venue, smoking, because of the no smoking indoors policies? Most often these people don't exude a lot of confidence. I grew up in a family where addiction was prevalent, so I understand addiction. A smoking addiction is sad because it diminishes self-confidence.

In the last chapter, I wrote about how emotional and environmental stress limits your highest genetic expression. The same holds true for telomeres. When you have your emotional and environmental stressors handled, you increase your opportunity to thrive through the decades.

4. Abusing alcohol. Alcohol abuse ages your cells and shrinks your telomeres. There are, however, limited ways alcohol can be beneficial. Red wine contains resveratrol, which can be antiaging and have other health benefits. Once you surpass one glass (or two at the most), the risks outweigh the benefits. I would never endorse anyone taking up drinking red wine to support telomeres, so if you don't drink, good for you. If you do drink, make sure you use red wine (or champagne or beer or tequila) in moderation. If you're abusing alcohol, then you are literally changing the way your body is aging at a cellular level.

SIMPLE TACTICS FOR HAPPY TELOMERES

Enough of the bad news. Let's get to the good stuff, including the lifestyle habits that will help make our telomeres long and strong, so we can live a long and healthy life.

Enjoy a plant-slant diet. This should sound familiar by now. I've presented the benefits of plant-slant nutrition for our inner pharmacy, our genetic expression, and overall health and performance. Remember the idea of nutrient density? Good health and longevity results from getting the most nutrients for the fewest calories. Plants deliver nutrient density while having few calories. Your cells will live long and strong with a plant-based diet. Does that mean you have to go vegan or vegetarian? No. What it does mean is that the vast majority of your calories should come from plants. As you know by now, I am a huge advocate for dark-green leafy vegetables as the bulk of your plate, and then you can include side-dish-sized portions for proteins and whole grains.

Move. Studies show that 30 minutes of daily exercise helps grow telomeres. Now you have another powerful motivator for a consistent movement practice.

Meditate. This is an opportunity to sit quietly and just breathe, be mindful, center, relax, and disconnect. When we are under the influence of a relaxation response engaged by our deep breathing, we're in a place of peace and presence. Your telomeres love meditation for those exact same reasons.

Start where you are. This isn't about having to sit for an hour a day unless you want to. The Dalai Lama says he meditates every day for an hour in the morning and an hour every night. "Unless," he says, "I am really busy, and then I meditate two hours in morning and two hours at night." When you're really busy, that's when you need to be that much more present.

Find a community of like minds. Studies show that telomeres thrive when we are surrounded by loving and supportive people. All of us have a family of origin and a family of choice—those people you spend a lot of time with. These are the people who nurture your soul and see your highest possibilities and help bring them forth. Along with being wonderful company, they also positively influence your telomeres. Motivational speaker Jim Rohn famously said that we become the average of the five people with whom we spend the most time. The meaning behind comes down to this: Who you hang out with and spend time with influences the person you ultimately become. These individuals can uplift you as much as they can bring out your worst qualities. Who are those people in your life?

Napping and sleeping. In addition to all the benefits of rest and deep, restorative sleep, you can add lengthening telomeres to the list of sleep benefits.

Journal Exercise: Your Lifestyle and Your Telomeres

Reflect on your lifestyle. Do you have changes to make in relationship to the four areas that shorten telomeres and diminish the health of your DNA (stress, sugar, smoking, and/or alcohol)?

Write down some ideas to help you reduce or eliminate stress (in addition to reducing sugar, smoking, and alcohol). Think meditation, journaling, walking, etc. Next, write about how you will support your telomeres and DNA with a plant-based diet, at least 30 minutes of daily exercise, meditation, and growing a community of like-minded people. Good for you if you are already making the most of your opportunities in these areas.

As you write, remember that we are talking about practice, not perfection. With practice you show up every single day for the great work of your life. Too often when we embrace personal development, we draw up a laundry list of all the things we are going to do, usually more than we can do at any one time. Then we beat ourselves up over what we don't check off the list at the end of the day. That kind of perfectionistic mind-set creates more stress and won't motivate us.

Being the architect to build the great masterpiece of your life is about practice, not being an overnight sensation. Have a sense of lightness as you record the changes you would like to make. For instance, play with a plant-based diet. Have fun. Find foods you love and discover ways of cooking and preparing healthy food you enjoy. Then eliminate the things about diet and cooking that don't work for you or cause too much stress.

Here are a few more ideas: How about a fun game of tennis in the morning and a hike in the afternoon? Add an after-dinner walk and you have great, fun daily exercise without the stress. Over time you will have cumulative benefits that are the product of a dedicated practice. Approaching these practices as fun means they will be sustainable.

Finally, evaluate your tribe. Does your inner circle love and affirm you? Do they bring out the best in you? Do you have energy vampires in your life? Vampires sap your vitality with negativity. They are toxic, engage in gossip, and lower your faith in humanity and your faith in yourself. You want a family of choice that lights up your spirit.

THE DEEPEST KIND OF SUCCESS

The practices in this chapter will allow you to create the deepest kind of success now and through the decades. Always remember you are alive to the degree that you serve. The more that you are wildly contagious with your self-love and your self-care, the more you will want to serve yourself and others every moment of your life.

CHAPTER NINE

The Secret to Having
Happiness and Success

Just in case happiness and living a healthier life are not enough motivation for you to follow this program, I want to share a secret with you. When you prioritize self-care, you will enjoy greater professional and personal success, plus real and lasting happiness. In essence, the entire Mind Body Life Mastery program is the practice of happiness. Isn't that a relief? You don't have to "try" to make yourself happy. Happiness happens naturally when you live in alignment with your character and integrity.

Our competitive culture teaches us that we need to be successful before we can be happy, but new research into the science of happiness tells us just the opposite. Being happy first makes success more likely. Happiness is not about material stuff. It's all about what you do each and every day. Self-efficacy—taking positive action for yourself and others—creates happiness. I know that this has been true in my life. There were times I was successful as a professional yet ultimately unhappy because I wasn't my best self around those I love. Perhaps you have felt the same way.

This chapter isn't about elation, or temporary pleasures, although there will be moments of both. This is about the deeper happiness that comes from living in a way that brings peace, purpose, and a feeling of being truly alive.

WHAT WE CAN LEARN FROM SUCCESSFUL AND HAPPY MILLIONAIRES

I don't want you to take my word alone about your opportunity to be successful and happy. Let's explore the habits of wildly successful, happy, and fulfilled individuals. I have presented at several of Robin Sharma's "Titan Summit" events, dedicated to mastery and peak performance. During one of the summits, I met Tom Corley, a financial planner and author of Rich Habits: The Daily Success Habits of Wealthy Individuals. Corley spent five years studying the habits of successful people and entrepreneurs. His research subjects included not only millionaires, but also billionaires.

Corley's personal life story includes both poverty and abundance, which led him to reinvent the way he looked at abundance. You see, Corley studied self-made millionaires and billionaires who were successful and happy, and not because of their financial abundance alone. These are people who know that stress takes them out of their game. These are people who prioritize quality of life alongside their business successes.

These successful and happy people share many habits in common with the ones I've outlined here. I humbly submit this mastery program that goes beyond what these wonderful people are doing, so you have a phenomenal opportunity to embrace happiness and quality of life alongside your professional success.

FIVE HABITS TO BUILD SUCCESS AND HAPPINESS

Habit 1: Read for at Least 30 Minutes a Day

These successful people read at least 30 minutes a day. And (hopefully) obviously, I am not talking about reading People magazine. Their reading is focused on personal development, human potential, business, and spirituality. They are continually learning to grow their lives. They read at least two books a month. That's 24 books a year to grow your life. Think about all you will have learned at the end of each month if you develop this habit. Reading opens your mind to lessons in living well. Lifelong learners create an amazing quality of life for themselves and those they love. The people Tom studied are just like you and me. Simply by reading this book, you are in a rare class. You are a student of your own life.

Habit 2: Trade TV Time for an Opulent Bubble of Positivity

Tom found that successful people watch an hour or less of television a day. As you know by now, I am not a fan of television in spite of the fact that I make part of my living on TV. Except for occasional streaming movies, I may watch about 5 to 10 minutes of television a day, and that is usually to catch up on my favorite sports teams. I'm clear that I'm not using my life at its highest level when I watch television.

With these practices, you are creating an environment that supports success at every level. This environment you are designing is an opulent bubble of positivity that protects and inspires you to thrive.

Think of your life like a garden. When you walk into a pristine garden, do you ever notice how one weed will stick out like a sore thumb? You want to pull it out. When you start designing a beautiful life day by day, you are going to notice what doesn't align with your own life's beauty. This is your opportunity to change what isn't in alignment.

Habit 3: Create a Window for Your Workouts

Successful people move and exercise every day for at least 30 minutes, at least five days a week. You have already learned about the importance of exercise for building the neurochemistry and energy for success. All motion creates positive emotion. Be present and focused during your workout.

I do a lot of traveling. I've seen people in hotel gyms in the morning. In between sets they are texting or reading emails. They are distracted. I give these people props for making it to the gym, but I want you to create an opulent bubble to focus solely on a world-class workout. Whether your workout is 5 or 45 minutes, set aside your phone! Your workout is about the sacred, great work of sweating, raising your heart rate, and aligning your inner pharmacy to make the most of the day's opportunities. You can't do that while checking emails or texting.

Habit 4: Get at Least Seven Hours of Sleep a Night

These successful people sleep at least seven hours a night. I do talks all over the world, and I see more people are adopting Western ideas of success and our driven lifestyle. This is translating into people from other nations becoming as sleep deprived as Americans. That means more stress-related diseases and life-threatening challenges are increasing around the world.

Don't postpone a good night's sleep until things slow down because that time is never going to come. Remember you are the architect of your life choices. Slow down today. At least seven quality hours of sleep gives you the opportunity to live an awesome life of service.

Habit 5: Get a Head Start on the Day

People who are successful in life and work wake up three-plus hours before their workday starts. If they start work at 7:00 a.m., they're up at 4:00 a.m. They spend these three morning hours reading, learning, and exercising. When you begin the morning practice described in this program, you join these happy, successful people making the most of their mornings. Do you see how critical the morning is? Let this sink in. As I wrote earlier, being a night owl is the result of habit and behavior, not your biology. You can change.

The best research on success and happiness shows morning people live the longest and strongest. They create momentum with a couple of key wins first thing in the morning, and that momentum leads them to their next wins. By early afternoon, they have a sense of peace because they accomplished the most important things that they needed to take care of by lunchtime.

What would it be like to have three hours (or even one hour) of focus on personal development, inner peace, and prosperity before work or before children? Before you can serve others, you have to serve yourself. I have seen too often, especially in the case of new parents, when we allow ourselves to fall further down the list of priorities. It may not be realistic, at least in the present moment, to find three hours for your personal development. But what if you could find one hour? What if you could devote 20 minutes for movement, 20 minutes for meditation and 20 minutes for personal growth (reading, journaling). Could you find an extra hour in the morning for that? If you don't go to work until 10pm and get home in the wee hours of the morning, can you take one hour for yourself and another 30 minutes to prepare a nourishing meal before crawling into bed?

BONUS HABIT: Carry a Notebook

Corley found that the most wildly successful people all carried journals and notebooks wherever they went. They know that some of their best ideas can pop up at any time. These can be ideas for being a better spouse, a better parent, or moving a business forward. By having a notebook with them at all times, they are ready to receive. Most importantly, during downtime they reread their insights and aha moments. They know how to step off the stress express, read their notes, and think about evolving their lives.

If someone says something profound or an insight comes, write it down. Go old school. Have a great pen or pencil close by at all times so you can put on paper those important thoughts that spontaneously drop in. Writing by hand engages learning and memory and provides that wonderful tactile sensation. With a notebook you are always prepared to be a student of your great life.

THREE PRINCIPLES FOR SUCCESS AND HAPPINESS

Tom found that his successful and happy research subjects use three principles to guide their lives: prioritizing relationships, saying no to requests that take them away from their highest priorities, and taking action.

1. Prioritize Relationships

Happy and successful people prioritize relationships. I've seen this in my own work and practice. Prioritizing relationships is the mark of true leaders in communities, companies, and families. Moving your circle of concern from "me" to "we" is the greatest way to create success, happiness, and mastery.

In earlier chapters, I wrote about ego-focused extrinsic motivation and service-oriented intrinsic motivation. People who are extrinsically motivated are more depressed, anxious, sleep less, and tend to be challenged in sustaining healthy relationships. Being concerned about fame, money, and status means we don't connect in a meaningful way with others and we constantly worry about the impression we are making.

The key to success and happiness is moving our focus from me to we. It's a win-win when we have a community of people we love. Everyone benefits. The way you show up can be a positive catalyst for everyone in your community. When you prioritize relationships, you will be amazed as you attract more opportunities, which in turn bring greater success, happiness, and fulfillment into your life.

A Pacific Medical Institute study looked at a group of men ages 50 to 70 years old who had a history of stress and other risk factors for heart disease. The study looked at whether there was a personality trait that predisposed some of these men to heart disease. The researchers taped their conversations and counted how many times they used first-person pronouns like "I" and "me" versus inclusive pronouns like "we" and "us." What they found was sobering. The men that spoke from a place of I and me had a much greater chance of developing heart disease than those who spoke from we and us.

In reading these results, I was reminded of constriction versus flow. When your focus includes we and us, there's flow and circulation of the good. When you're self-focused, there's constriction. It is incredibly liberating to shift your focus from me to we. Watch your use of pronouns as a measure of your focus.

In that same vein, people who create success in every area of their life are listeners rather than talkers. They listen and they ask important and appropriate questions. They don't get their self-confidence from needing to be right or by having to be the ones talking all the time.

2. Learn to Say No

You may be familiar with the Jim Carrey movie, *Yes Man*. The film's moral was supposed to be that saying yes leads to openness to life and abundance. In my life, I am learning it is possible to say yes too often. The masters of success are also masters of respectfully saying no.

They maintain boundaries to focus on what is really important and meaningful to them and aligned with their greater purpose. They say no to requests that are not in alignment with their agenda for the day, week, or year. And they don't feel bad about it. They feel excited by their opportunities.

This does not mean you can't say yes. A practice that I have found helpful is to create windows in my week or month specifically for service. Set aside times when you can mentor or volunteer. This is wonderful. I want you to do that. But outside of those windows, create protected space within your opulent bubble. Be focused. Don't let demands or requests from others take you out of your game plan. The more awesome you become, the more requests are going to flood in. Dedicate yourself to what you know works. You serve no one by sacrificing your self-care.

Peace of mind depends on becoming a master of saying no when appropriate and living the Mind Body Life Mastery system. On the other hand, if your mind is busy, if you feel you missed out on important things, or you fell short on your commitments, it's probably because you didn't honor yourself. You weren't in integrity with what you want to be standing for.

It takes incredible courage and self-respect to say no. When you do say no, you not only respect yourself, but your life and your goals. You help make this self-care system sing on your behalf.

3. Take Action and Affirm Optimism

Successful people believe in themselves and their abilities. They take action. This goes back to the principle of self-efficacy. Self-efficacy, happiness, and optimism all go hand in hand. Think about it: When you're feeling optimistic and happy, it's because you have a belief in yourself to act and influence events. Your confidence will grow as you take action for your self-care and self-awareness. As you take action in all areas of your life, you develop optimism and confidence. This is not an intellectual process. It is a physical, emotional, and spiritual experience.

Optimism has a wonderful physical side effect: it lowers inflammation. Think about that. The more that you look at life with optimism, the more you decrease the cytokines, those compounds that drive inflammation. Inflammation makes you stupid. Inflammation makes you fat. Inflammation makes you depressed. Inflammation will make you all the things that you don't want to be. If you are not feeling optimistic about your ability to take action and be a positive influence, you will miss out on mastery's most important physiological elixir.

Journal Exercise: How Can You Incorporate These Three Principles?

Being happy and successful begins right here, right now, by taking action. Write about what you can do with these three principles. How can you support your relationships? How can you move your focus from "me" to "we"? How can you listen more and talk less? Next, write down demands that are distracting you from your A game. Being a master of saying no will get you the greatest yeses, the yeses that allow you to create what you came here to create. This is the awesome experience of dedicating yourself to the architecture of success.

As you do this exercise, you are taking action and gaining confidence in your ability to improve your life, so get specific about how you will implement these principles. You build optimism by deciding what action step to take and doing it. Ideas and vision are important, but we must also take it to the next level by acting and producing. It's like going from being an amateur to a pro. As writer and screenwriter Steven Pressfield says in his book *The War of Art*, "Turning pro is a mind-set. If we are struggling with fear, self-sabotage, procrastination, self-doubt, etc., the problem is, we're thinking like amateurs. Amateurs don't show up. Amateurs crap out. Amateurs let adversity defeat them. The pro thinks differently. He shows up, he does his work, he keeps on truckin', no matter what."

This act of journaling as self-love has the wonderful side effect of decreasing systemic inflammation. Plus, your positive emotions will spill over to the people you know and even people you don't know as it ripples out as an emotional contagion. Knowing this provides intrinsic motivation.

RANDOM ACTS OF KINDNESS SPREAD HAPPINESS

Now let's look at some of the ways the Mind Body Life Mastery program goes beyond what Tom found in his research. This program, by its very nature, builds happiness, thereby providing you the foundation for success in all parts of your life.

Kindness is at the heart of being a ruckus maker. Random acts of kindness are a way of raising happiness for you and everyone around you who sees your acts of kindness. Happy people inspired by your act proceed to move throughout their social circles influencing the mood of everyone they come in contact with; and those people in turn influence people you have never even met in ever widening circles.

Kindness unleashes our inner pharmacy. First, being kind and witnessing kindness increases endogenous opioids, which are natural painkillers. As these opioids increase, a burst of bliss is experienced. Second, dopamine levels increase in the kindness giver and receiver. You improve your motivation and the motivation of others, by your loving actions; not your talk. Third, oxytocin, the love chemical, increases in giver and receiver. You experience the benefits of oxytocin when you give someone a great big hug. Oxytocin has cardiovascular benefits and helps to lower blood pressure. So, when you are experiencing a kindness, you and the recipient experience decreased stress, which may improve cardiovascular health. Kindness may also lead to increases in serotonin, the brain chemical of calm and well-being, also known as the happiness hormone. Strong serotonin levels lead to more resilience. You don't know what is going to come at you moment to moment in life, but if you have a good store of serotonin, you will regain your balance more quickly when confronted with an unfortunate surprise or act.

Practicing kindness helps to normalize the stress hormone cortisol, which left unchecked may shorten life span and contribute to inflammation. Exercising kindness may decrease C-reactive protein, a blood marker for chronic systemic inflammation.

I really want you to see the connection between kindness and lower levels of inflammation. Kindness is not simply a frivolous afterthought when you are setting your goals and intentions for the day; it is a powerful force for good in the world. If you want to build happiness, consider being very intentional about a daily practice of kindness. This one practice will influence how your day and your life will unfold.

Let's make this idea even more practical. Say you are working and your dopamine is down so your focus and motivation are lagging. Choose an opportunity to do a kind act for someone. It is the perfect antidote when you feel self-defeated or like you are losing your mojo. By thinking of others, you change the game physiologically, spiritually, and emotionally not only for you, but for so many other people. You are alive to the degree that you serve.

Journal Exercise: Random Acts of Kindness

Think about five people whom you can influence over the next seven days with an act of kindness, and write down one thing you can do for each person. Here are some ideas: Send an appreciative email, text, or a fun picture. If you know they have a routine place where they are every day, surprise them there and offer a kindness. Buy a stranger a cup of coffee. The results of this practice are so great, yet the practice itself can be simple and lots of fun. Be passionate about your kindness practice.

MIND BODY LIFE MASTERY BUILDS HAPPINESS

Let's look at how your other Mind Body Life practices are already building your happiness.

Remember the "best life" practice from chapter 1 where you reflected on where you want to be 5, 10, and 15 years down the road? I invite you to do this practice often, at least once or perhaps twice a year. Studies show that when we undertake a best life reflection we grow our happiness in the present. It's a win-win because we are wiring our brains to embrace our highest future vision, which, in turn, makes us happy now.

The best life practice also helps us be more thoughtful about what we want to bring into our lives. Create an autobiography for your life to come. Read it as a part of your spiritual practice before you meditate or pray. Read it out loud for even more energy. This is a powerful practice that is scripting out what you want to create in your life.

The practices of healthy nutrition, meditation, exercise, and all the things that we have explored in this book build happiness. Prioritizing self-care can seem counterintuitive in this culture. We've been taught that self-care is selfish, that we need to put others' needs ahead of our own. My friends, the opposite is true; self-care gives us the energy and passion to be of much greater service to our families, our communities, and the world.

Another mastery practice scientifically shown to increase happiness is writing in a gratitude journal. This is a cornerstone for not just building greater happiness, but improving sleep as well. The benefits of gratitude have been researched for more than 30 years, so you can trust those results will be there for you.

And while we're in the gratitude mind-set, let's add forgiveness to our list of mastery practices. Research into the power of forgiveness shows that the act of forgiveness shifts our neurochemistry positively and liberates our spirits. The outcome of forgiving is greater happiness for you. You aren't excusing bad behavior but instead having compassion for human frailties and releasing the hold that others' acts have had on your mind and body.

Three additional Mind Body Life Mastery practices have a positive impact on growing happiness. They include:

Setting and pursuing goals.

Belonging to a spiritual community.

Relationships that include abundant, genuine appreciation for others. It is a great joy and honor to love, encourage, and support someone else. You are supporting your physiology and spirit, and theirs as well.

Building happiness is a success principle. We make our immune systems stronger, our energy more vibrant, and find purpose and passion that elevate every area of our lives. Your dedication to being the highest expression of you brings greater happiness into your life and into the lives of all those around you.

WHAT MAKES US UNHAPPY?

Comparing ourselves to others is a major driver of unhappiness. When we try to keep up with what others have or copy what they do, we become unhappy. This provides the science behind the popular warning against "keeping up with the Joneses."

Releasing the need to compare your life with anyone else's can be incredibly freeing. Imagine using your energy to focus on how to improve your service to others and live your highest expression, instead of keeping track of who has achieved what.

The poison of social comparison is fueled on social media. We are bombarded with information about people we may not even know doing awesome things, getting promotions, and visiting exotic places. Our lives may seem dull and boring by comparison. We must realize we are seeing a tiny fraction of their lives. Everyone has challenges and unexciting parts to their lives, but they don't post those things and neither do we. Be really clear that comparing yourself to others on social media usually results in unhappiness.

Journal Exercise: Scheduling Your Happiness Practices

Answer these questions:

What 12 books will you read this year?

If you watch television, what programs are you willing to let go of to gain more time for self-care, happiness, and mastery?

What time will you schedule your workout windows?

How much sleep are you getting currently? Are you well rested? What are three steps you can take immediately to improve your sleep?

What time do you wake up? How will you create more time in the morning to build your day?

You may already be doing many of these practices. If you are, good for you. If you are not, don't beat yourself up. Be a student of your great life. Now take some time to schedule happiness practices into your day. Be realistic. Will you wake up a bit earlier? Will you give up an hour of television or social media scrolling? Write it down.

EPILOGUE:

Embrace Practice, Not Perfection

As a father of two daughters, I have come to realize that they are my greatest teachers. The first thing I want to do when I see them is to appreciate them before I do anything else. I want to be loving and present for them before I go into the smaller dad that's demanding, "Clean your room," "Do this," or "Do that." That is not the feeling I want to leave them with.

Think about a loved one. Think about a person in your life where you can rework those moments to first express appreciation to those you love.

We think of a legacy as something we leave behind after we die, such as money or a memoir. The reality is that we are leaving a legacy every single moment of our lives. Your interactions with others are either loving or less than loving. Every interaction, no matter how simple, leaves a legacy.

Reflect on that new definition of legacy as you think about your life after reading this book. In the introduction, I invited you to live a great life that brings together success, happiness, and meaning. Being aware of your moment-to-moment legacy is the key to bringing together success and happiness.

What kind of legacy will practicing Mind Body Life Mastery allow you to leave in your life, not just for yourself but for everyone around you? Be mindful that every interaction that you encounter with another leaves a legacy. That simple awareness is how you use all this book's information to support your life purpose. Becoming a mindful student of the power of your great life moves you into the exceptional space of world-class performance in your living and giving.

WHAT IS THE CYCLE OF A GREAT LIFE?

You will find your great life when you grow, fail, get back up, learn from that failure, and grow again. That one word—fail—can cause considerable discomfort. We are so attached to not failing. We are so attached to wanting to know everything. We think we will be safe and others will not see our insecurities if we know everything. Let me tell you, no one knows how it's all done. I invite you to fail.

Disciplined students of living aren't perfect, but they still serve and create a phenomenal legacy. Be a disciplined student of your own life, and notice when your legacy in each moment is loving or when it is not loving. When it isn't where you know it could be, you have found the learning opportunity in the grow-fail-grow cycle.

Avoid perfectionism as you implement the exercise and self-care plan in this book. Take an honest look at where you might be holding onto the idea that you have to know everything about mastery or that you have to do these practices perfectly on the first try. You know what? You will never be finished creating your great life. Test these practices and find out which work the best for you. Trying and experimenting with anything in life is the source of true happiness and fulfillment.

Perfectionism never brings happiness, but it does increase our risk for depression. We are bound to be sad because we know we can't continually be awesome. Eventually we are likely to fail.

Since failure is inevitable, why not embrace it and gently ask ourselves, without judgment, what we can learn from the experience. Learning from failure and growing in wisdom increases our happiness.

Perfectionism raises the risk for heart disease. Consider this metaphor. Our hearts are a place of love. We don't practice self-love and compassion when we are gripped by perfectionism. Our hearts suffer as a result. That realization was a wake-up call for me. At times in my life I believed I couldn't allow myself to be imperfect. Under the spell of perfectionism, I felt like my heart ached. The metaphor is literally true—our heart does ache, and heart disease can follow if our performance is driven by perfectionism.

Tal Ben-Shahar, a popular writer and Harvard professor, talks about "optimalism." Optimalism is not optimism. It's the idea of always being open to our higher expression by learning how to do things better every time. Optimalism is knowing that what may be your best performance today may not be the same tomorrow. It is the best you can do in that moment. As long as you show up and give your all, you can always learn from your performance. Optimalism is the key to embracing the grow-fail-grow cycle. Practicing an optimalism mind-set contributes to happiness, decreases inflammation, and increases longevity. Optimalism supports Mind Body Life Mastery and being a student of your great life.

YOU CAN'T ALWAYS CLIMB THE MOUNTAIN

In your mastery practice you will encounter plateaus, periods where you can't see any noticeable improvement. Just as you can't always be perfect, you can't always be climbing the mountain. There will always be peaks and valleys.

Our society conditions us to look for a series of ecstatic moments, one after the other. Think about beer commercials. The actors are shown exercising, then hanging out with friends, and then partying. You see all these sensational moments in 30 seconds. The message is that life is always about being awesome and experiencing sensational moments.

Life mastery is not built through a series of never-ending highs. When you are experiencing a plateau in your practice, draw on your grit and be persistent. Practice is all about sustaining your focus. Use the plateau to keep refining your craft. Excellence in Mind Body Life Mastery is demonstrated in your willingness to be positive and keep working in the plateau. Every now and then, you are going to improve your performance or have an "aha" realization that's going to take you to the next level. Please understand that you will never reach the next level if you don't have the grit to use the plateau to continue the work. Your legacy is built working in the plateau to achieve great moments, and from those great moments, you learn how to take your life to the next level. Then you start the process anew.

 Journal Exercise: Perfectionism versus Optimalism

Reflect on your relationship to perfectionism. Are there some areas of your life where you have more perfectionism than other areas? How can you replace any areas of perfectionism with optimalism? Give yourself permission to be a student of your great life. Life can always become greater if you allow yourself to fail and grow.

BUILDING RESILIENCE AND WILLPOWER FOR LONG-TERM MASTERY

Let's look at some practices to build resilience and boost your willpower. Both resilience and willpower will be essential to you to sustain the Mind Body Life Mastery program in the plateaus and throughout your life.

THREE CORE RESILIENCE PRACTICES

Resilience is everything when it comes to achieving great success and creating a legacy. You can't achieve mastery without embracing life's plateaus. You have to know how to be on that plateau and be wonderfully awake to the opportunities in each and every moment. That shouldn't be daunting, it should be seen as exciting.

1. Resilience is built on intervals. We've talked about intervals both in relationship to exercise and managing your energy during the work day. The lesson in both those applications is understanding that "sprinting" in any part of your life needs to be accompanied by resting. During the workday, be "on" for 52 minutes and "off" for 17 minutes. Be dedicated and live your A game and then make sure you know when it's time to rest and recover. Sustained life mastery requires mastery of interval pacing in all areas of your life.

2. Uni-task. You will never achieve mastery when you are trying to do two or three things at once. You are not at your best when you are juggling too many balls in the air. I used to fall prey to trying to do several things at once. I now understand that uni-tasking—focusing on one thing at a time—yields the highest quality work. I am also clear that my happiness and peace of mind depend on uni-tasking.

When you multitask, your brain never gets the chance to experience success. Think about it. When you finish one thing, you immediately replace that task with the next task, and you do it again and again. You never get a chance to say, "Good for me," or feel a sense of accomplishment or completion before moving onto the next task. Denying your brain that sense of completion can lead to depression and increased anxiety. Neurologically, your body feels like you never get anything done. You feel like a slacker even though you may be accomplishing many tasks. Uni-tasking will rewire your brain for better focus, higher performance, and greater happiness and fulfillment because you stop to savor your successes.

3. Bookend your day. The morning bookend is about waking up and taking care of yourself. Remember one of the secrets of successful, happy people: they get up three hours before they go to work. Before they jump into their work, they practice self-care. Then they go throughout the day performing at the top of their game before they have another bookend in the evening, resting and connecting with loved ones before bed. Bookending your day is a lot like unitasking. By bookending you realign with purpose and passion on either side of being a human doing.

These three practices will build resilience for the plateaus and help sustain your Mind Body Life Mastery practice moving forward. Your success isn't about your GPA or IQ. It's much more about your ability to sustain your energy and focus, perseverance, and tenacity.

THREE SIMPLE WILLPOWER PRACTICES

How else can we ride the plateaus with greater purpose and passion? We do it by exercising willpower practices associated with grit. These three simple practices are core to this program, as they ignite your willpower and willingness, allowing everything else to fall in place.

1. Breathe well throughout the day. How? Make sure you are using your diaphragm. Breathing well is the foundation for being awake, mindful, and present to be a student of your great life. Diaphragmatic breathing reduces inflammation and cortisol. It helps you perform at a high level.

2. Move first thing in the morning and throughout the day. Movement will keep your neurochemistry and physiology humming while boosting willpower and grit.

3. Eat at regular intervals to sustain energy and blood sugar.
To sustain willpower and grit, your brain requires a steady flow
of glucose. You are not at your best when your brain is running on
fumes. We have to be mindful of taking time throughout the day to
keep our brain nourished. When our brain is nourished, our focus
and motivation are sustained.

Every single day remember to breathe, move, and eat well. Everything
else will flow from these core practices. Doesn't that make it simple?

Journal Exercise: Building Grit to Achieve Your Goals

Pick three primary life goals. Reflect on how building your resilience, grit, and willpower by breathing, moving, and eating well
will allow you to make those goals a reality.

Mind Body Life Mastery is about being awake every moment to
what you need, how you can serve, and how you can show up as
your best self. The great psychologist Abraham Maslow said it so
well: "What we can be, we must be." How do you accomplish
that? Self-care and self-awareness are simple but not easy. The
first step is to have a foundational system in place like Mind
Body Life Mastery. Then you build grit—being absolutely deter-
mined and focused on showing up every moment as a student
of your great life, a life that is always evolving into ever greater
expression.

LIVING YOUR LIFE WITH NOBLE PURPOSE

Aristotle talked about eudaemonia, meaning "to live your life
with noble purpose." We now know that serving with nobil-
ity lowers inflammatory body chemicals that drive mortality,
disease, and depression, and undermine success.

Living with noble purpose helps create your legacy by being awake to possibility moment to moment. There are 86,400 seconds in your day. Each one of these seconds is an opportunity to show up and leave a loving legacy.

When you think about what is it you want to be doing from this moment forward, consider the power of focusing on your noble purpose. Purpose is about spirit, heart, and soul. Focusing on outcomes brings up the ego. Did I do it perfectly? How do I look in others' eyes? Instead, whether you win or lose, focus on how you showed up. Did you embody your noble purpose? How can you express even more of your highest potential next time?

The Mind Body Life Mastery program is a guide to help you embody the mastery that you already possess by embracing the grow-fail-grow cycle. These practices and tools support what you came into this world to do. You came here to be a eudaemonist, a ruckus maker, to live life on fire with purpose and passion. That is legacy. That is a life well lived.

Cut away all that is not in alignment with your highest expression of living and giving. Let it fall away and find the courage and commitment to move into your highest possible expression in each moment. Let growth be your normal state of being.

This is our time to rise and shine and create a ruckus. This movement begins with you, it begins with me, and it begins right now.

The legacy that we leave gives rise to everything we want to see in our world. We can help create a cultural contagion to wake up everyone around us. In this movement, we are the leaders, the catalysts, and the courageous change makers. All of us have the opportunity to as Gandhi famously said, "be the change we wish to see in the world."

Much love and many blessings on your journey. Thank you for the opportunity to serve your highest expression. I am grateful to you for stepping up and serving the entire world around you. This is your time.

APPENDIX

Mind Body Life Mastery Supplements

Are you in a place where you know that you can absolutely show up every single day and eat impeccably? If you can, good for you. But for a lot of us, that's going to be tough. We all have busy lives. If you travel, like me, there are always those circumstances where you can't eat as healthfully as you would like. Supplements may help to fill the gaps and serve as a sort of "insurance policy" when our lifestyles and meals aren't what we would like them to be. You don't have to take all these supplements every day. If you are eating wild fish a few times each week and eating nuts and seeds or using a good quality ground flax or flaxseed oil, you may not need to supplement daily with omega-3s, for example.

Supplements complement healthy dietary choices. First focus on making food choices that truly nourish your body. We can't lean on supplements to overcome a poor diet. Diet is absolutely the foundation of Mind Body Life Mastery. Check with your health care provider to make sure the supplements that you're considering are in alignment with your individual health needs and compatible with other medications and supplements you may be taking.

MY PERSONAL FAVORITE DIETARY SUPPLEMENTS

Consider the following to support optimum mental and physical energy.

Acetyl-L-carnitine may just be my favorite supplement. It builds protein and boosts memory, focus, and mental energy. It can help with the challenges of age-related cognitive decline and keeps your mind functioning at an optimum level. This is a tremendous supplement for all of us who face cognitive demands at work. The average recommended dose is 500 mg (milligrams) to 1500 mg daily.

Alpha-lipoic acid is a safe, well researched, and powerful antioxidant designed to reduce inflammation and increase energy. Sometimes called ALA, the recommended dose is between 50 mg to 100 mg, two to three times a day. You can take 50 mg or 100 mg with breakfast, lunch, and dinner, or consider just taking it at breakfast and lunch if you don't need a lot of energy later in the day.

Coenzyme Q10 (CoQ10) occurs naturally in every cell in your body and synergizes with other biochemicals to generate cellular energy. Stress, poor diet, and lack of exercise lower CoQ10 levels (as do statin drugs). Supplementing with 100 mg of CoQ10 one to three times a day is a great way to support your mitochondria. CoQ10 is particularly important if you are using statin drugs to control cholesterol since statins tend to deplete CoQ10.

D-ribose is a favorite supplement of athletes. I endorse it if you are looking for something to increase energy for your morning workout. The average recommended dose is 5 mg to 10 mg daily.

Magnesium performs more than 300 jobs inside of the body, including manufacturing energy, balancing blood sugar, supporting heart muscle, and reducing painful muscle contractions. If you are stressed or a perfectionist, your magnesium levels may be low. If you don't sleep well, your energy is off, you crave sugar, or you get those painful cramps in your calves, consider taking magnesium. Ever get freaked out when your eyelid starts to twitch? Much of the time that's due to low magnesium. Studies show that 70 percent of

Americans are deficient in magnesium. Look for chelated magnesium glycinate, which is better absorbed by the body. (Other forms of magnesium [like citrate] tend to go straight to your bowels causing loose stools.) Consider 400 mg to 500 mg of chelated magnesium glycinate a day. I like to take 200 mg to 250 mg in the morning and the same dose at dinner or bedtime. This pattern may help sleep quality.

Some of my other favorite supplements below may assist your highest genetic expression and the ability to thrive through the decades, among many other benefits.

Ashwagandha is an Ayurvedic herb—a rasayana, or tonic. As an adaptogenic herb (meaning it adapts to the need of the organism), ashwagandha benefits the entire body and mind, and its range of use is quite broad. Remember the mind state of equanimity from our exploration of meditation? The more we practice meditation and mindfulness, equanimity allows us to find our way back to center quicker when we get off base. I think of ashwagandha as the equanimity herb. When our cortisol is running crazy high or crazy low, ashwagandha helps get us back to that place of balance. There is also evidence that ashwagandha is useful for endurance exercise and fitness as well as improved coordination. The dose is generally 1 g (gram) to 3 g daily.

Glutathione is the "queen" of your antioxidant army. When glutathione levels are strong, all the other antioxidants light up. Glutathione is the catalyst for a phenomenal antioxidant cocktail to fight free radicals and protect your telomeres, DNA, and cells. Glutathione supports the immune system and helps protect against certain cancers and chronic diseases such as type 2 diabetes, heart disease, dementia, Alzheimer's disease, asthma, and autoimmune disease. It is found in dark-green, leafy vegetables, avocados, and whey protein powder. Make sure your whey protein powder is derived from grass-fed cattle, without growth hormones. And if you don't yet love avocados, glutathione is another reason to learn to love this beneficial food. Glutathione changes the game for your health, longevity, performance, and overall well-being. Quercetin also boosts glutathione, so be sure to review that entry in this appendix section.

Omega-3 fatty acids build a strong foundation for gene support as well as long and strong telomeres to help you age well. Omega-3 fats are concentrated in the brain (and are essential in developing brains) and maintain nerve cell membrane structure. Insufficient omega-3 fatty acid intake is linked to poor memory and depression. There was an interesting study, published in the American Journal of Clinical Nutrition, that demonstrated how daily supplementation with omega-3 fatty acids (1.8 g of eicosapentaenoic acid [EPA] and docosahexaenoic acid [DHA]) actually altered genetic expression of over 1,000 genes, with notable decreases in genetic expression of genes that are involved in inflammation in the body. (Reference: M. Bouwens, O. van de Rest, N. Dellschaft, et al., "Fish-Oil Supplementation Induces Anti-inflammatory Gene Expression Profiles in Human Blood Mononuclear Cells." American Journal of Clinical Nutrition 90 [August 2009]:415-24.)

In choosing an omega-3 supplement, the first thing to consider is the amount of EPA and DHA in each gelcap or capsule (vegetarian sources are available, however, vegetarian sources generally have lower concentrations of EPA and DHA). You will see many opinions as to the ideal ratio of EPA:DHA. It is often set at about a 2:1 ratio, most specifically for the benefits to heart health (lowers inflammation, blood pressure, and cholesterol levels). I tend to go against the grain here and opt for a higher DHA compared to EPA. This looks something like 1000 mg DHA to 220 mg EPA. I am a big fan of the cognitive, anti-inflammatory, and cardiovascular support that DHA offers, though it is a bit pricier than EPA.

Dietary sources of omega-3s include wild salmon and other wild fish, nuts and seeds, avocado, and ground flax meal. But with the growing concern of mercury along with other toxins in our seafood sources, supplementation may be a strong consideration, and I always recommend researching the supplement company to make sure that they test all of their products for toxins and/or heavy metals. A good online source to estimate the amount of mercury that you may be ingesting is: https://seaturtles.org/programs/mercury/.

Quercetin is a dietary flavonoid (a.k.a. bioflavonoid), which is part of a pigmented (colored) family of compounds found in virtually all plants. Flavonoids are responsible for most of the brilliant yellow, orange, and red pigments of fruits and vegetables and function as antioxidants in the body. Quercetin has powerful antioxidant, anti-inflammatory, anticancer, antibacterial, antifungal, antiallergic, and antiviral properties. Quercetin occurs naturally in many common foods and beverages, including red wine, apple and onion peels (especially red onions), berries, buckwheat, green tea, and, to a somewhat lesser degree, red grapes, citrus fruits, tomatoes, broccoli, leafy greens, cherries, raspberries, cranberries, and other fruits and vegetables.

One of my favorite things about quercetin is that it helps the body produce glutathione, the "queen" of antioxidants (see above). Quercetin also has an antihistamine effect, which can be beneficial for individuals with allergies.

Evidence from human studies suggest that quercetin may have a positive effect on physical endurance and performance. As a result, quercetin may offer potential advantages for athletes and individuals looking for increased endurance and energy. It can also help the body recover from a workout. The dose can vary depending on usage, but a typical daily dose would be 1 g to 2 g.

Turmeric is one of my favorite food supplements and I consume it every day. It is a powerful superfood in the form of a small root (Curcuma longa) that has been used medicinally around the world for thousands of years. With origins in India, turmeric root, whether whole or powdered, has been featured in Asian cuisine, cosmetics, and medicine and is recognized for its bright yellow pigment (be aware, it will stain cutting boards and clothing). As medicine, it is probably most widely used as an anti-inflammatory agent. It is also used as a digestive aid. Recent studies have demonstrated turmeric's activity against developing cancers (in particular, cancers of the skin, breast, stomach, and oral cavity). Other research is looking at turmeric as a possible preventive agent in the development of Alzheimer's disease.

University of California Los Angeles Medical School has been studying turmeric for more than 22 years for its relationship to brain health, mental well-being, fighting inflammation, and helping to extend life. They have found that turmeric is phenomenal for supporting our cells and genetic expression.

Turmeric is more effective when you take it with a little fat. What I love to do is combine a heaping teaspoon of turmeric with a little black pepper and a tablespoon of raw, organic coconut oil. The oil is almost like jelly. The fat from the coconut oil and the black pepper help absorb the turmeric. I put it on the stove on very low heat to let everything melt together. Once melted, it's boom, down the hatch. What a wonderful way to start your day. The healthy fat provides medium-chain triglycerides for energy, the turmeric fights inflammation, and you start your day as a ninja! You are barely out of bed and your brain and body are saying, "Woo-hoo! We are off to the races." I am psyched just writing about it.

Vitamin D3 is essential to your health and genes. Most of us do not get adequate Vitamin D3 through diet alone, since very few foods actually contain vitamin D, unless we mainline fish for every meal (which I do not recommend). And although the sun is a great natural source of D3, with the fear of skin cancer many of us avoid the sun like the plague. Vitamin D3 plays a vital role in immune health, heart health, mental-emotional well-being, bone health, sleep—the list goes on. Most practitioners will check vitamin D3 levels with your annual blood work, so I recommend you ask your doctor about that if you haven't had your levels checked. You want to be in a place that's absolutely rock-solid. Dosing will vary depending on where your D3 levels are.

MORE SUPPLEMENT OPTIONS

I almost always take digestive enzymes with betaine hydrochloride with every meal. I also often take a probiotic, which is especially helpful to balance gut bacteria since I travel nearly every week. I also love phosphatidylserine (which supports cognitive function and memory and can lower cortisol).

I'm really into beets for endurance and as a pre-workout food. Beets can also help speed recovery after a workout. I designed two supplements based around beets including a pre-workout endurance blend (Endurance Beet Blend) for my company, Healthy Skoop.

I have also created a plant-based protein product called Breakfast Protein, which is a combination of plant-based proteins plus adaptogenic herbs, fiber, probiotics with an organic fruit and vegetable blend. In addition, I have formulated a powdered superfood and greens-based product called A-Game Plant-Based Greens Blend, as well as Sleep Protein powder—a first in its category—which has a blend of proteins, complex carbohydrates, and nutrients to support sleep. For more information on any of these supplements, visit www.healthyskoop.com.

RECOMMENDED READING

As I've mentioned, I am a voracious reader. I wanted to share a list of some of my favorite books for personal development, leadership, spirituality, and mastery.

Altruism by Matthieu Ricard

The Motivation Manifesto by Brendon Burchard

Originals: How Non-conformists Move the World by Adam Grant

Love 2.0: Creating Happiness and Health in Moments of Connection by Barbara L. Fredrickson, PhD

Tools of Titans: The Tactics, Routines, and Habits of Billionaires, Icons, and World-Class Performers by Tim Ferriss

Think and Grow Rich by Napoleon Hill

Autobiography of a Yogi by Paramahansa Yogananda

The Compound Effect by Darren Hardy

Bhagavad-Gita As It Is by A. C. Bhaktivedanta Swami Prabhupada

Flow: The Psychology of Optimal Experience by Mihaly Csikszentmihalyi

The Code of the Extraordinary Mind by Vishen Lakhiani

The Science of Mind by Ernest Holmes

A Path with Heart: A Guide through the Perils and Promises of Spiritual Life by Jack Kornfield

The Four Agreements: A Practical Guide to Personal Freedom by Don Miguel Ruiz

The Greatest Secret in the World by Og Mandino

ACKNOWLEDGMENTS

A book on mastery is never written alone. Many family and chosen family members have all contributed to this expression through their love, belief, and outright leading of the heart. I wish to gratefully appreciate my dream team of creative co-conspirators and courageous ruckus makers from across the planet: Dan Sims; J Madden; Rob Coleman and Team THRIVE; Al Moscardelli; John Allen; Scott and Laura Carlin; Greg Wells; Geoff McIntosh; Kevin Dooley; Betsy Wiersma; Cathy and Gary Hawk; Lauren Miller; Bobby Macauley; Lauren Matthews Langtim; Ned Brown; Kevin and Colleen McFadden; Chuck Coyle; Mike Urness; Adam Greenburger; Rob Bennet; Alex Bogusky; Rob Schuham; Fred Harmon; Jim Quandt; Evan Mann; Kevin Snook; Rebecca and Jan Hermann; Kristina Karlsson; Rishi Khemka; Ashwin Vijay; Harry Korras; The Novak family; Tom and Dawn Terwilliger; Cynthia James; Carl Studna; Roger and Erica Teel; my Dr. James Rouse Facebook community; my Well and Company tribe; and my SKOOP tribe. It is a gift and a blessing to have had the honor of working with talented co-conspirators on this project. Sonja Sweeney, I am so grateful for you and your brilliant copy-editing. Harv Bishop, thank you for organizing my thoughts, my words, and speaking my language. Thanks to Bruce Pfrommer for designing the book cover to cover. And to my inspiring, courageous, brilliant, and beautiful wife, Dr. Debra; and Dakota and Elli Rouse—thank you for being a source of love and light that has always been a force for courage, commitment, and all-out desire to bring passion and purpose into everything that I do now and always, xoxoxoxoxoxo. May your path be one of heart that inspires a desire for mastery in all that you do and all that you pursue.

ABOUT THE AUTHOR

Dr. James Rouse is passionate about helping people thrive and develop the high performance lives they deserve. He has written 13 books including *Think Eat Move Thrive: The Practice for an Awesome Life; Essential Practices for Living an Extraordinary Life;* and the award-winning *Colorado Fit Kitchen: Inspiring Recipes for Mind, Body, Beauty, and Optimum Wellness*, coauthored with his wife, Dr. Debra Rouse. Dr. James is a highly sought after international speaker with engaging messages on leadership, self-care, connection, life mastery, and service. He is a life coach and trainer, having studied and mastered leading edge human performance strategies for over 30 years. As a naturopathic doctor and serial entrepreneur, he has launched and leads a multimedia company (Optimum Wellness), has founded several companies in the nutrition and nutriceuticals space, and continues to develop leading-edge nutritional products. For more information visit www.drjamesrouse.com.

CPSIA information can be obtained
at www.ICGtesting.com
Printed in the USA
FSHW011031211020
75078FS